M000272610

DESIGNS OF NATURE

ENTWÜRFE DER NATUR
DISEÑOS DE LA NATURALEZA
DISEGNI DI NATURA
FORMES DU MONDE NATUREL

DESIGNS OF NATURE

ENTWÜRFE DER NATUR
DISEÑOS DE LA NATURALEZA
DISEGNI DI NATURA
FORMES DU MONDE NATUREL

THE PEPIN PRESS

Copyright for this edition © 1997 The Pepin Press B/V

Copyright introduction 'Designs of Nature' © 1997 The Pepin Press B/V

First published in 1997 by The Pepin Press

Edited and produced by Dorine van den Beukel

ISBN 90 5496 042 6

The Pepin Press

POB 10349 • 1001 EH Amsterdam • The Netherlands

Tel (+) 31 20 4202021 • Fax (+) 31 20 4201152 • E-Mail pepin@euronet.nl

Printed in Singapore

Designs of Nature

Throughout history, nature has been a source of inspiration for artists and designers. Rock paintings dating back to prehistoric times show pictures of people, animals and plants. Since then, most cultures have used nature's forms for ornamentation, either because of the symbolic value attributed to some animals and plants or purely for decorative purposes.

Each culture had its own favourite plants and animals. In ancient Egypt, for instance, animals featuring often in ornamentation were the sphinx, the scarab, and the sparrowhawk. The most important plant motifs were derived from the lotus, papyrus and palm. These continued to be used in Greek decorative arts, where they were further developed into the palmette motif (see page 147). However, the main Greek plant motif was the acanthus, which for centuries has been popular in a whole variety of styles (see pages 56-59). The Romans added the festoon to the palmette and acanthus motifs, a garland of flowers and fruit hanging in a curve and held together by ribbons (see page 11). Acanthus leaves and the palmette motif continued to be used during the Romanesque period, albeit in a highly stylized form. In the Gothic era, floral motifs became even more popular for a wide range of applications, varying from the illumination of manuscripts to the decoration of cathedrals. Typical shapes included maple, oak, lime, ivy, chestnut, vine, thistle, strawberries, tulip, and violet. The animal shapes used in ornamentation were mostly fabulous creatures or monsters, such as the gargoyles on Gothic buildings. During the Renaissance, artists returned to the classic motifs. Shells, coral and stalactites were motifs added during the Baroque period. The acanthus remained popular in combination with floral compositions. By the end of the 18th century Asian flower patterns had become very popular, and Napoleon's Egyptian Campaign resulted in the adoption of Egyptian plant and animal motifs such as the lotus and the sphinx.

The Romantic Movement of the early 19th century gave rise to a widespread admiration for all aspects of nature. At the same time, in accordance with Christian doctrine, God was seen as the Creator of all living things. The publication of Darwin's *On the Origin of Species* in 1859 drastically altered man's view of nature, providing an enormous impulse to scientific research. As a reaction to increasing industrialization and mechanization, the emphasis on representations of nature in the arts increased even more. This development reached its zenith in the Arts & Crafts Movement and the Art Nouveau style, which were both characterized by their highly stylized designs inspired by nature. An incredible number of Asian and European plants and animals were depicted, many of which are to be found in or near water: swans, cranes, water-lilies and lotuses.

This book contains mostly 19th-century material, and offers the unique combination of realistic, scientific drawings and stylized ornaments. The contents of the book can be divided into plants and plant ornamentation (pages 13-170) and animals and animal ornamentation (pages 171-336). The first section includes cells (pages 50-51), foliage (pages 54-65), mushrooms and other spore-bearing plants (pages 44-45, 68-77), and fruits (pages 38-43). The animal section includes bacteria (page 45), mammals (pages 171-237), birds (pages 238-277), amphibians and reptiles (pages 278-289), fish (pages 290-301), insects and spiders (pages 302-315), and crustaceans and molluscs (pages 316-335).

Entwürfe der Natur

Schon immer war die Natur eine wichtige Inspirationsquelle für Künstler und Designer.
Prähistorische Felsmalereien zeigen Darstellungen von Menschen, Tieren und Pflanzen. Später
verwendeten die meisten Kulturen natürliche Formen für Ornamentik, sei es aufgrund der
symbolischen Bedeutung einiger Tiere und Pflanzen, oder sei es für rein dekorative Zwecke.
Dabei hatte jede Kultur ihre bevorzugten Pflanzen und Tiere. Im alten Ägypten beispielsweise
waren die Sphinx, der Skarabäus und der Sperber in der Ornamentik häufig verwendete
Tiermotive. Die wichtigsten Pflanzenmotive waren Lotusblume, Papyrus und Palmen. Dies
setzte sich auch bei den Griechen fort, die sie in Ihren Verzierungen zum Palmettenmotiv
(s.S. 47) weiter entwickelten. Aber das dominierende griechische Planzenmotiv war der
Akanthus, über Jahrhunderte und in vielen Stilvarianten beliebt (s.S. 56-59). Die Römer fügten
eine bogenförmige, aus hängenden Blumen und Früchten, von Bändern (s.S. 11) zusammen-
gehaltene Girlande in das Palmetten- und Akanthusmotiv ein. Akanthusblätter- und
Palmettenmotive wurden in der Romanik weiter verwendet, wenn auch in äußerst stilisierter
Form. In der Gotik erfreuten sich Blumenmotive in vielen Anwendungen noch größerer
Beliebtheit, vom Illustrieren von Manuskripten bishin zum Verzieren von Kathedralen. Die häu-
figsten Blumenmotive waren Ahorn, Eiche, Linde, Efeu, Kastanie, Weinrebe, Distel, Erdbeere,
Tulpe und Veilchen. Bei den Tieren traten hauptsächlich Fabelwesen oder Ungeheuer auf, wie
zum Beispiel die Wasserspeier auf den gotischen Gebäuden. In der Renaissance griffen die
Künstler auf klassische Motive zurück. Das Barock bereicherte mit Muschel-, Korallen- und
Stalaktitenmotiven. Akanthus blieb in Verbindung mit Blumenmotiven weit verbreitet.
Am Ende des 18. Jahrhunderts waren asiatische Blumenmuster sehr beliebt, und in der Folge
von Napoleons Ägyptenfeldzug wurden ägyptische Pflanzen- und Tiermotive wie Lotus und
Sphinx übernommen.
Mit der Romantik im frühen 19. Jahrhundert entwickelte sich eine grenzenlose Bewunderung für
alle Bereiche der Natur. Gleichzeitig wurde, in Übereinstimmung mit dem christlichen Glauben,
Gott als der Schöpfer aller Wesen gesehen. Nachdem Darwin im Jahre 1859 sein Werk *Über den
Ursprung der Arten* veröffentlichte, änderte sich das Naturverständnis der Menschen grundle-
gend und es kam zu einem enormen Aufschwung in der Forschung. Als Reaktion auf die
zunehmende Industrialisierung und Mechanisierung verwendete man in der Kunst noch
häufiger und bewußter Naturformen und Darstellungen aus der Natur. Diese Entwicklung er-
reichte ihren Höhepunkt in der *Arts & Crafts* Bewegung und im Jugendstil, dessen hochstili-
sierten Formen und Motive der Natur entsprangen. Zahlreiche Motive asiatischer und europäi-
scher Flora und Fauna, viele aus dem Wasser oder mit dem Wasser verbunden, wurden verwendet: Schwäne, Kraniche, Seerosen und Lotusblumen.
Dieses Buch gibt hauptsächlich Motive aus dem 19. Jahrhundert wieder, und zwar in einer
einzigartigen Kombination aus realistischen, wissenschaftlichen Zeichnungen und stilisierten
Ornamenten. Das Buch ist unterteilt in Pflanzen und Pflanzenornamentik (Seiten 13-170) und
Tiere und Tierornamentik (Seiten 171-336). Der erste Teil umfaßt Zellen (Seiten 50-51), Blätter
(Seiten 54-65), Pilze und andere Sporenträger (Seiten 44-45, 68-77) und Früchte (Seiten 38-43).
Der zweite Teil stellt Bakterien (Seite 45), Säugetiere (Seiten 171-237), Vögel (Seiten 238-277),
Amphibien und Reptilien (Seiten 278-289), Fische (Seiten 290-301), Insekten und Spinnen
(Seiten 302-315) und Schalentiere und Weichtiere (Seiten 316-335) dar.

Formes du Monde Naturel

La nature a été une source d'inspiration pour les artistes et les designers tout au long de l'histoire. Les peintures rupestres remontant aux temps préhistoriques représentent des figures humaines, animales ou végétales. Depuis ce temps là, la plupart des cultures ont utilisé des figures de la nature, soit en raison de la valeur symbolique attribuée à certains animaux et à certains végétaux, soit dans un but purement décoratif.

Chaque culture possédait ses plantes et ses animaux favoris. Dans l'Egypte ancienne par exemple, les animaux souvent représentés dans l'ornementation furent le sphynx, le scarabée et l'épervier. Les principaux motifs végétaux étaient dérivés du lotus, du papyrus et du palmier. Ceux-ci continuaient à être utilisés dans les arts décoratifs Grecs où ils étaient plus largement développés dans le motif du palmier (voir p. 147). Cependant, le motif végétal Grec le plus important était l'acanthe, populaire depuis des siècles dans une grande variété de styles (voir p. 56-59). Les Romains ont ajouté un feston aux motifs de palmier et d'acanthe, une guirlande de fleurs et de fruits suspendus en courbe et maintenus ensemble par des rubans (voir p. 11). Les feuilles d'acanthe et le motif du palmier furent encore en usage durant la période Romane, mais dans une forme hautement stylisée. A l'ère Gothique, les motifs floraux devinrent encore plus populaires pour un large éventail d'usages variant de l'enluminure des manuscrits à la décoration des cathédrales. Les formes typiques comprenaient l'érable, le chène, le citron, le lierre, la chataîgne, la vigne, le chardon, les fraises, la tulipe, et la violette. Les figures animales utilisées pour l'ornementation étaient essentiellement des créatures fantastiques ou des monstres, tels que les gargouilles sur les bâtiments gothiques. Durant la Renaissance, les artistes revinrent aux motifs classiques. Au cours de la période Baroque, les coquillages, les coraux et les stalactites furent des motifs supplémentaires. L'acanthe restait populaire combinée à des compositions florales. A la fin du dix-huitième siècle, les motifs floraux asiatiques étaient très en vogue et l'adoption des motifs animaux et végétaux tels que le lotus et le sphinx fut un résultat de la campagne égyptienne Napoléonienne.

Le mouvement Romantique du début du dix-neuvième siècle fait croître une admiration répandue pour tous les aspects de la nature. Simultanément, en accord avec la doctrine chrétienne, Dieu était conçu comme le créateur de toutes les choses vivantes. La publication de l'ouvrage de Darwin – *Sur l'Origine des Espèces* – en 1859 a radicalement altéré la vision humaine de la nature, produisant une énorme impulsion dans la recherche scientifique. L'emphase des représentations de la nature dans les arts prit d'autant plus d'ampleur en réaction aux poussées de l'industrialisation et de la mécanisation. Ce développement a atteint son zénith avec le mouvement de l'Artisanat et le style de l'Art Nouveau, lesquels étaient caractérisés par des dessins fortement stylisés inspirés par la nature. Un nombre impressionant de plantes et d'animaux asiatiques et européens étaient représentés, dont la plupart étaient trouvés dans ou au bord de l'eau: cygnes, grues, nénuphars, lotus.

Ce livre contient pour la plupart de la documentation du dix-neuvième siècle, et offre une combinaison unique de dessins réalistes, scientifiques et d'ornements stylisés. Le contenu de cet ouvrage peut être divisé entre plantes et ornementation végétale (p. 13-170); animaux et ornementation animale (p. 171-336). Le premier chapitre comporte les cellules (p. 50-51), le feuillage (p. 54-65), les champignons et autres plantes à spores (p. 44-45, 68-77) et les fruits (p. 38-43). La section des animaux comprend les bactéries (p. 45), les mammifères (p. 171-237), les oiseaux (p. 238-277), les amphibies et les reptiles (p. 278-289), les poissons (p. 290-301), les insectes et les araignées (p. 302-315), les crustacés et les mollusques (p. 316-335).

Disegni di Natura

Nel corso dei secoli la natura è stata fonte di ispirazione per artisti, disegnatori e progettisti. Le pitture rupestri, che risalgono all'era preistorica, raffigurano persone, animali e piante. Quasi tutte le culture che si sono succedute da allora fino ai nostri tempi hanno utilizzato per la decorazione forme tratte dalla natura. Spesso l'interesse per queste forme era puramente ornamentale, ma in molti casi ha giocato un ruolo importante al valore simbolico che si attribuiva a certi animali e piante.

Ogni cultura ha avuto le sue preferenze in fatto di piante e animali. Nell'antico Egitto, per esempio, erano frequenti le raffigurazioni di sfingi, scarabei e sparvieri, mentre i motivi di origine vegetale più importanti erano quelli derivati dal loto, dal papiro e dalla palma. Il loro uso fu trasmesso all'arte decorativa greca, che ne sviluppò il motivo della palmetta (v. pag. 147). Ma nell'arte greca il motivo di origine vegetale più importante è stato quello, diffusissimo, dell'acanto, che da secoli è presente in tutta una varietà di stili (v. pagg. 56-59). Alla palmetta e all'acanto i romani hanno aggiunto il festone, una ghirlanda di fiori e frutta che pende incurvandosi verso il basso sostenuta da fasce (v. pag. 11). Le foglie di acanto e il motivo della palmetta sono rimasti in uso durante il periodo romanico, benché in forma molto stilizzata. Però nel periodo gotico sono stati superati in diffusione dai motivi floreali, che hanno trovato una vasta gamma di applicazioni, dalle miniature dei manoscritti alla decorazione delle cattedrali. Tra le piante che hanno fornito alla decorazione forme tipiche abbiamo l'acero, la quercia, il tiglio, l'edera, il castagno, la vite, il cardo, la fragola, il tulipano e la viola. La maggior parte delle forme di animali ricorrenti nella decorazione erano esseri mitici o mostri, come le 'gargolle' che scaricavano l'acqua piovana dalle grondaie degli edifici gotici. Durante il Rinascimento gli artisti ritornarono ai motivi classici. Conchiglie, coralli e stalattiti si sono aggiunti al repertorio dei motivi nel periodo barocco. L'acanto ha continuato a godere di grande fortuna in composizione con altri motivi floreali. Verso la fine del Settecento incomincia la fortuna delle forme tratte da fiori asiatici, mentre alle campagne di Napoleone in Egitto dobbiamo l'adozione di motivi egizi tratti da piante e animali quali il loto e la sfinge.

Il Romanticismo del primo Ottocento ha ispirato una diffusa ammirazione per tutti gli aspetti della natura, attraverso la quale, in armonia con la concezione cristiana, Dio era visto come il Creatore di tutti gli esseri viventi. La pubblicazione del libro di Darwin *L'origine della specie*, del 1859, ha alterato drasticamente la visione che l'uomo ha della natura, dando un enorme impulso alla ricerca scientifica. Come reazione alla crescente industrializzazione e meccanizzazione abbiamo nelle arti un accentuato interesse per la rappresentazione della natura. Questo fenomeno ha conosciuto il suo culmine nell'Arts & Crafts Movement e nello stile Art Nouveau, ambedue caratterizzati dal disegno estremamente stilizzato ispirato dalla natura. Vi furono rappresentati in numero incredibile piante e animali asiatici ed europei, con una notevole presenza di quelli che popolano le acque e le sponde: il cigno, la gru, la ninfea e il loto.

La maggior parte del materiale contenuto in questo libro risale all'Ottocento e comprende una combinazione unica di disegni realistici, scientifici, e di ornamenti stilizzati. Il contenuto del libro può essere diviso in piante e motivi ornamentali vegetali (pagg. 13-170) e animali e motivi ornamentali zoomorfi (pagg. 171-336). La prima sezione tratta cellule (pagg. 50-51), foglie (pagg. 54-65), funghi e altre crittogame (pagg. 44-45, 68-77) e frutti (pagg. 38-43). La sezione degli animali comprende batteri (pag. 45), mammiferi (pagg. 171-237), uccelli (pagg. 238-277), rettili e anfibi (pagg. 278-289), pesci (pagg. 290-301), insetti e ragni (pagg. 302-315) e crostacei e molluschi (pagg. 316-335).

Diseños de la Naturaleza

A lo largo de la historia, la naturaleza ha sido fuente de inspiración para artistas y creadores. En las pinturas rupestres de los tiempos prehistóricos, encontramos imágenes de personas, animales y plantas. A partir de entonces, la mayoría de culturas han utilizado como ornamento las formas y diseños que ofrece la naturaleza, ya sea debido al valor simbólico atribuido a ciertos animales y plantas o con intenciones meramente decorativas.

Cada civilización tiene sus plantas o animales predilectos. En el Antiguo Egipto, por ejemplo, los animales utilizados con más frecuencia eran la esfinge, el escarabajo y el gavilán. En cuanto a los ornamentos vegetales, predominaban los inspirados en plantas como la flor de loto, el papiro y la palmera. Éstos encontraron continuación en las artes decorativas griegas, donde, posteriormente, se desarrollaron y adquirieron características propias (véase la página 147). No obstante, el acanto fue la planta preferida por los griegos, y mantuvo su popularidad durante siglos, llegando a adoptar una gran variedad de estilos (véanse las páginas 56-59). Los romanos añadieron el festón a los motivos del acanto y la palmera; éste consistía en una guirnalda en forma curva compuesta por flores y frutas unidas entre sí por medio de cintas (véase la página 11). Las hojas de acanto y la palmera continuaron utilizándose durante el románico, aunque estilizaron su forma. En el período gótico, el uso de los motivos florales se extendió a otros ámbitos, desde el embellecimiento de manuscritos a la decoración de catedrales e incluyeron hojas de arce, roble, lima, hiedra, castaño, parra, cardos, fresas, tulipanes y violetas. Las figuras de animales más utilizadas en ornamentación eran criaturas fantásticas y monstruos, como las gárgolas que encontramos en los edificios de la época. Durante el Renacimiento, los artistas retornaron a los motivos clásicos. Con la llegada del barroco, se introdujeron otros motivos como las conchas, el coral o las estalactitas, mientras el acanto conservaba su popularidad, aunque combinado con composiciones florales. A finales del siglo XVIII, los diseños de flores asiáticas habían adquirido una gran popularidad, y la campaña de Napoleón en Egipto trajo como consecuencia la adopción de motivos de animales y plantas típicamente egipcios, como la flor de loto y la esfinge.

El movimiento romántico de principios del siglo XIX, desarrolló una profunda admiración por la naturaleza en todos sus aspectos y, al mismo tiempo, y en concordancia con la doctrina cristiana, resaltó la figura de Dios como Creador de todos los seres vivos. Cuando en 1859 se publicó *El origen de las especies*, la teoría de Darwin alteró drásticamente la visión que el hombre tenía de la naturaleza, y proporcionó un impulso enorme a la investigación científica. Ante la influencia cada vez mayor de la industria y la mecanización, el tema de la naturaleza se extendió con más fuerza que nunca dentro de las artes. Este proceso alcanzó su máxima expresión con el movimiento de las Arts & Crafts y el modernismo, ambos caracterizados por la estilización de unos diseños que se inspiraban en la naturaleza. Se representaron un gran número de plantas y animales asiáticos y europeos, la mayoría de los cuales eran acuáticos o estaban en estrecha relación con el agua: cisnes, grullas, lirios de agua y flores de loto.

El material que contiene este libro pertenece principalmente al siglo XIX, y ofrece la combinación única de ornamentos realistas, dibujos científicos y diseños estilizados. El contenido del mismo puede dividirse en: plantas y ornamentación floral (páginas 13-170) y animales y ornamentación animal (páginas 171-336). La primera sección incluye células (páginas 50-51), follage (páginas 54-65), hongos y otras plantas portadoras de esporas (páginas 44-45, 68-77) y frutas (páginas 38-43). La sección de animales incluye bacterias (página 45), mamíferos (páginas 171-237), aves (páginas 238-277), anfibios y reptiles (páginas 278-289), peces (páginas 290-301), insectos y arácnidos (páginas 302-315) y, por último, crustáceos y moluscos (páginas 316-335).

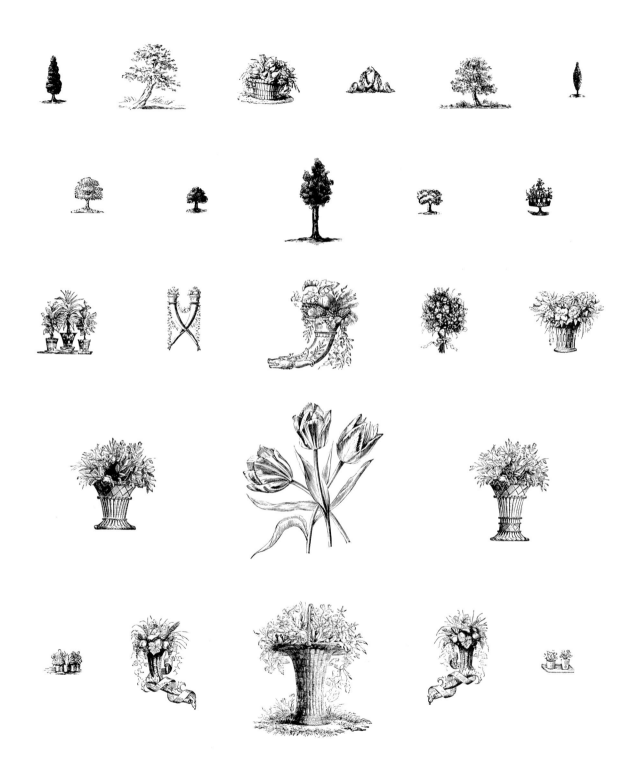

16

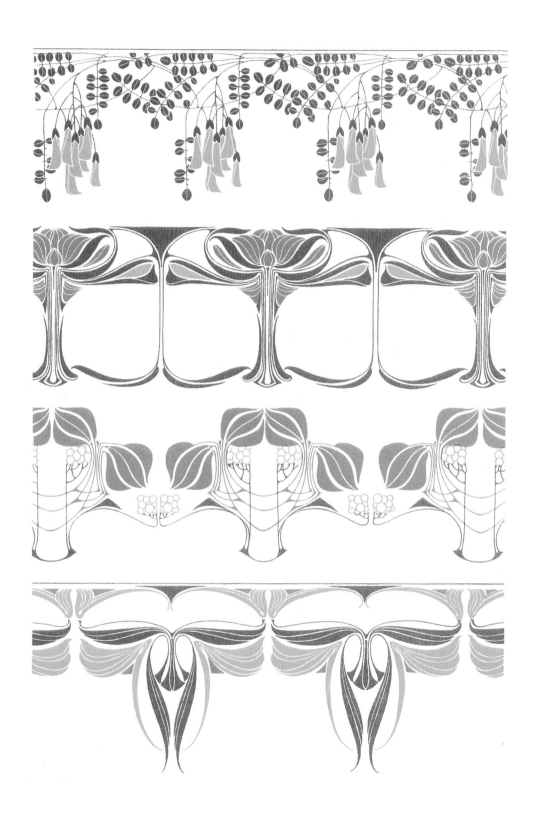

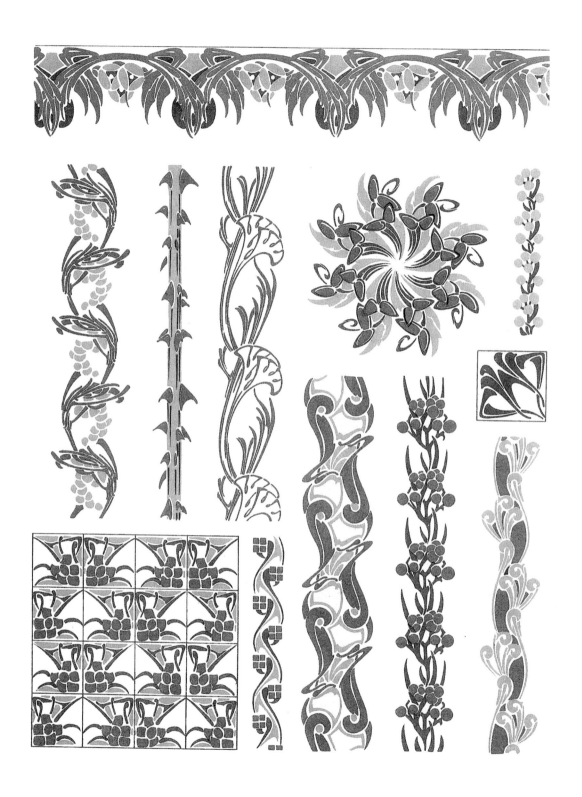

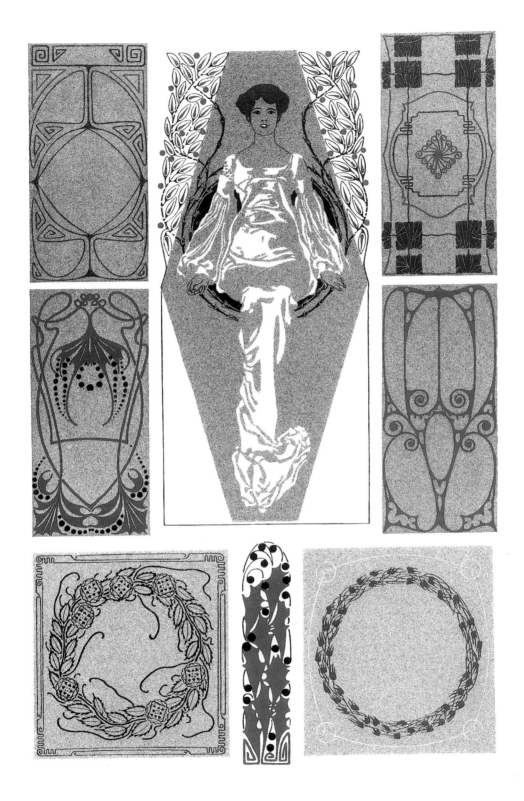

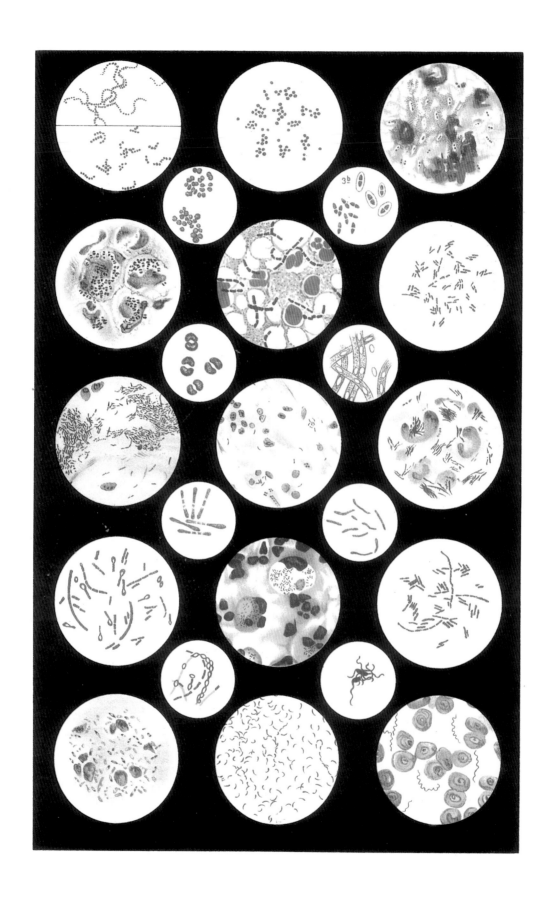

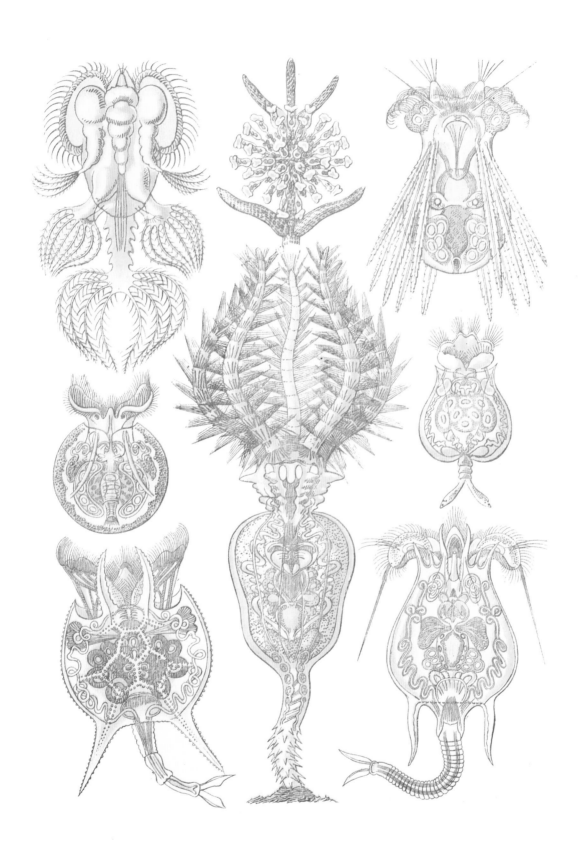

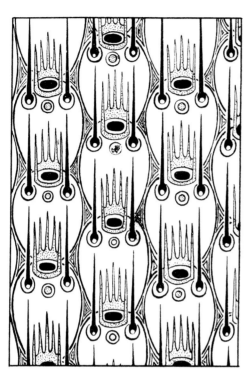

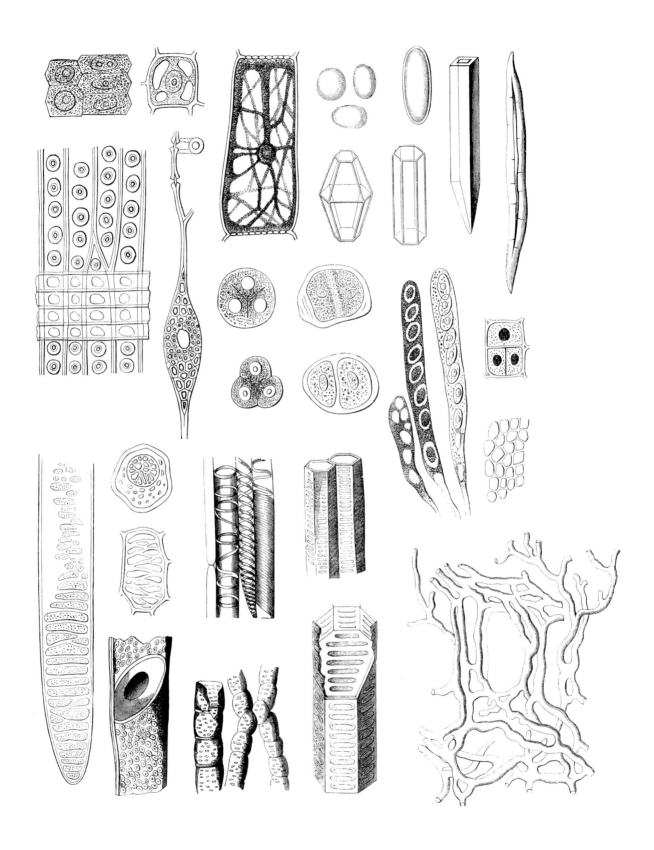

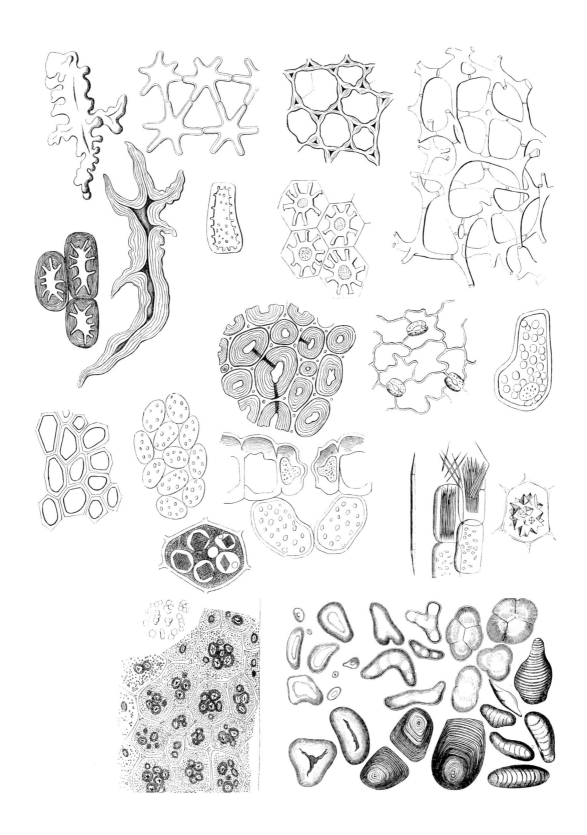

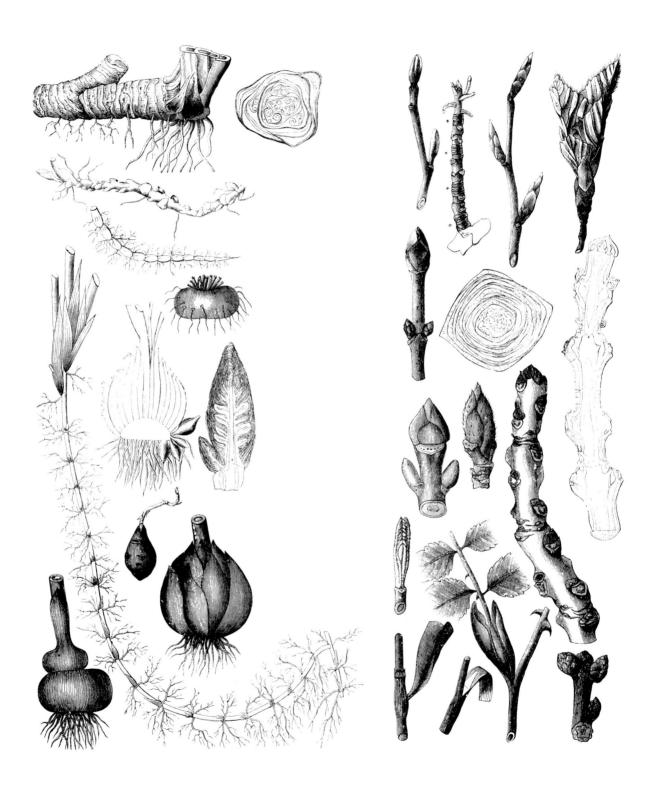

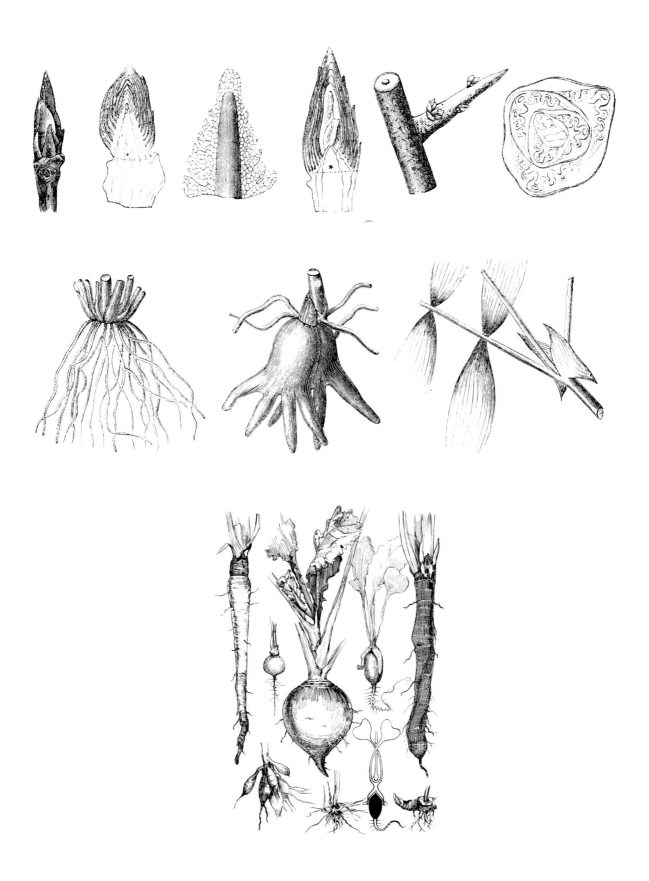

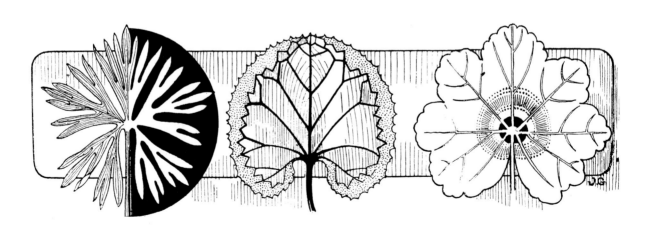

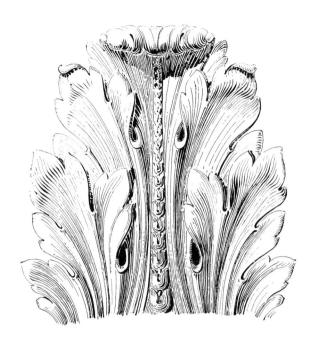

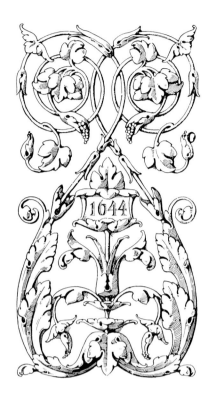

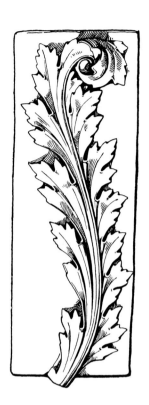

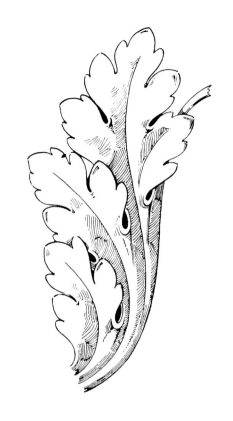

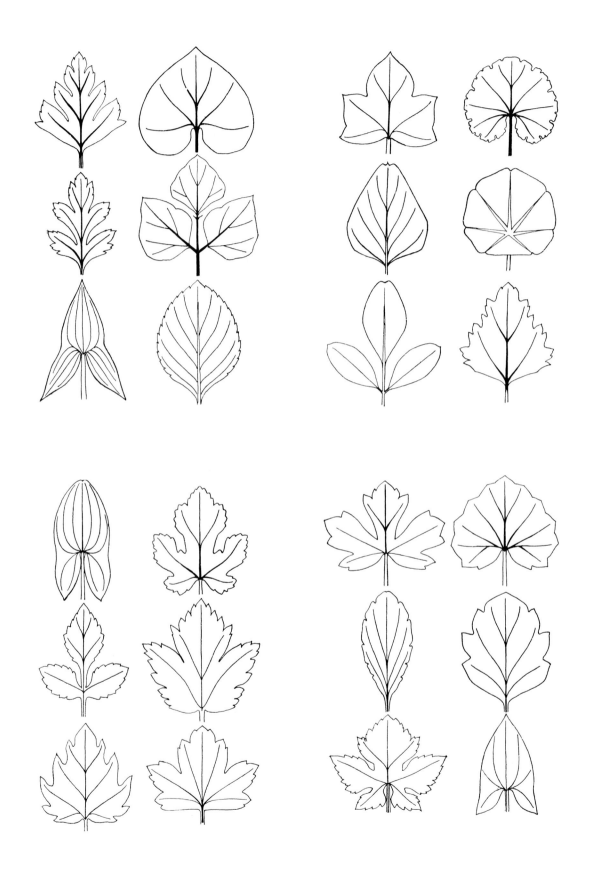

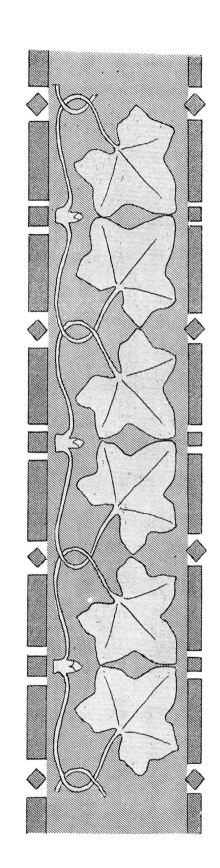

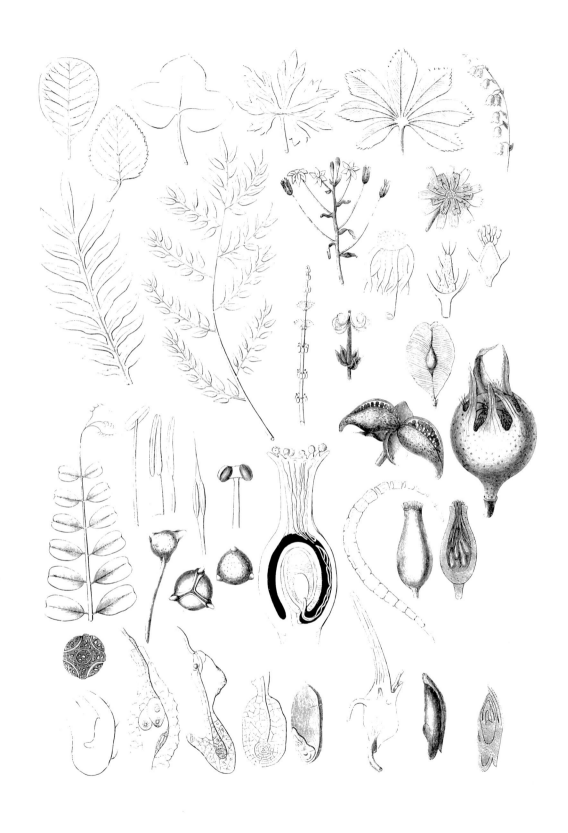

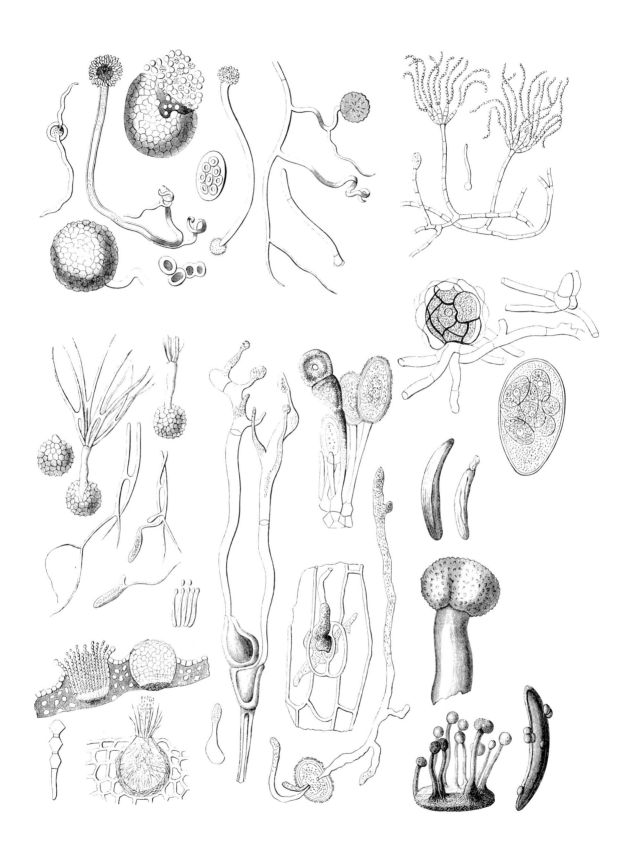

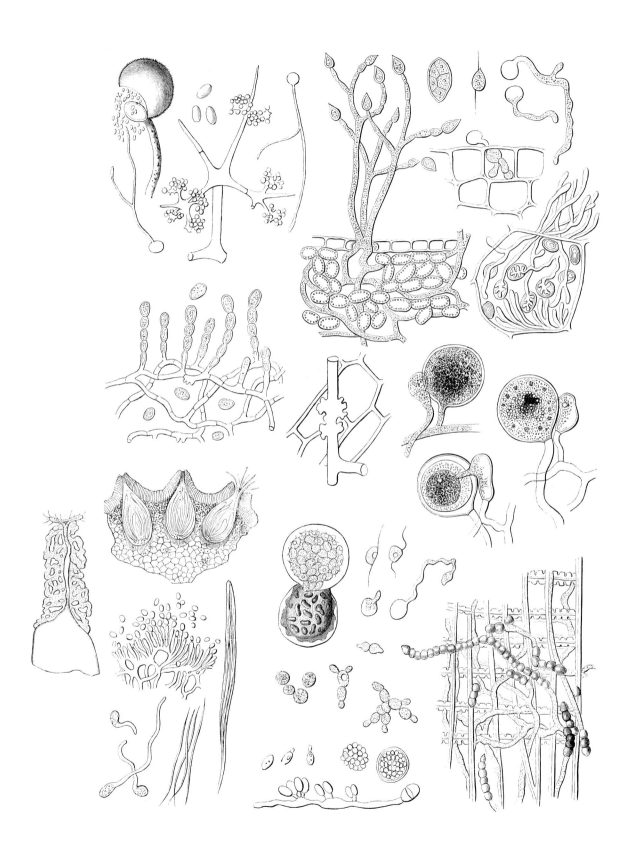

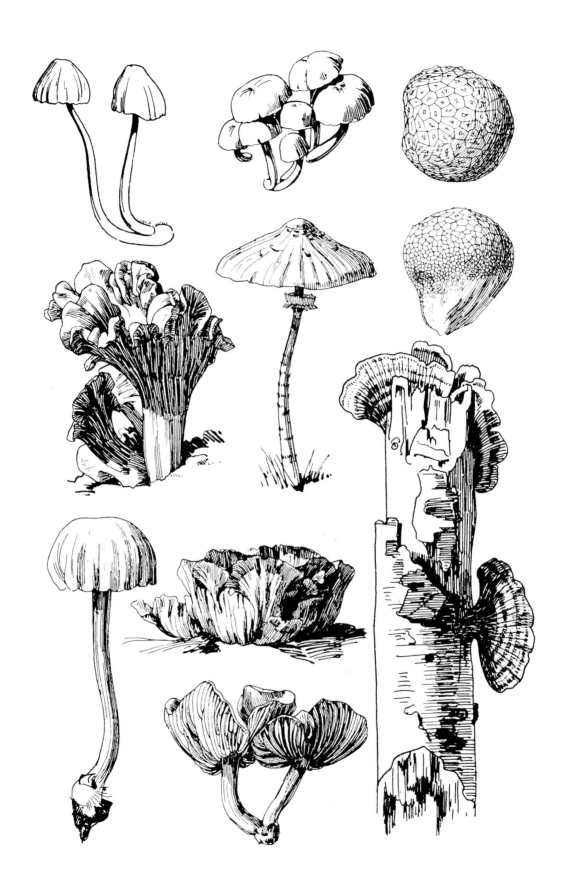

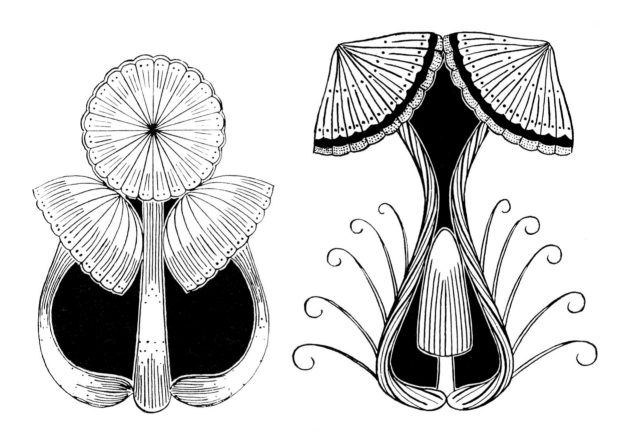

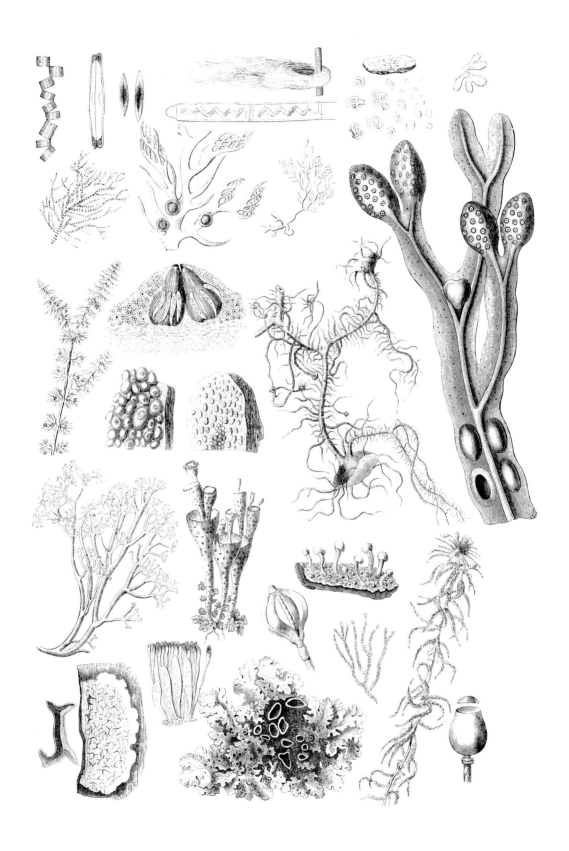

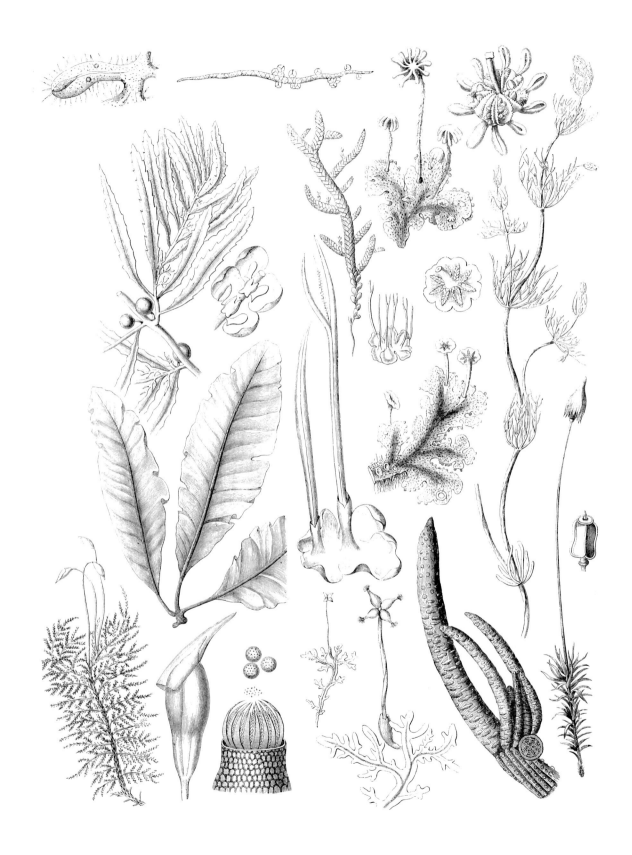

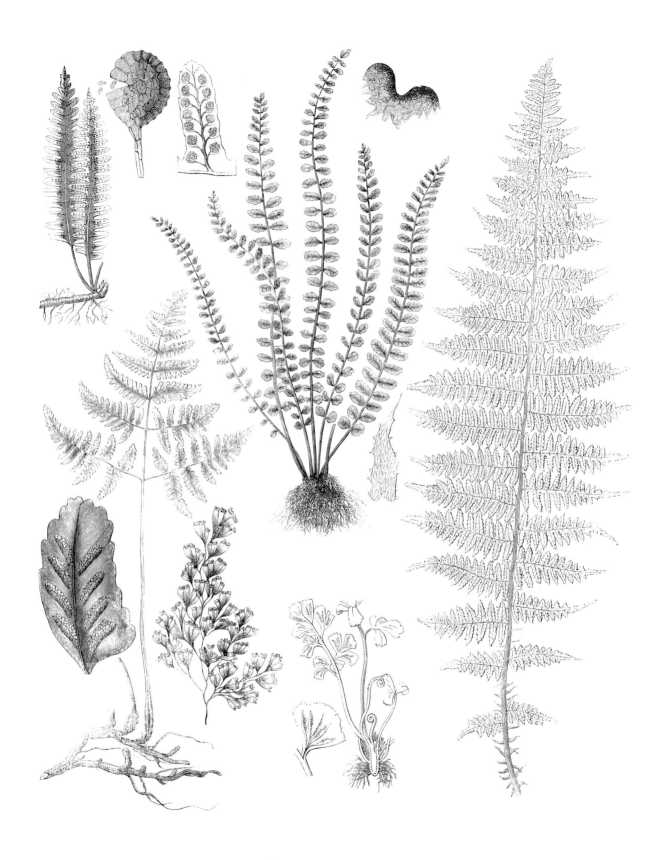

72

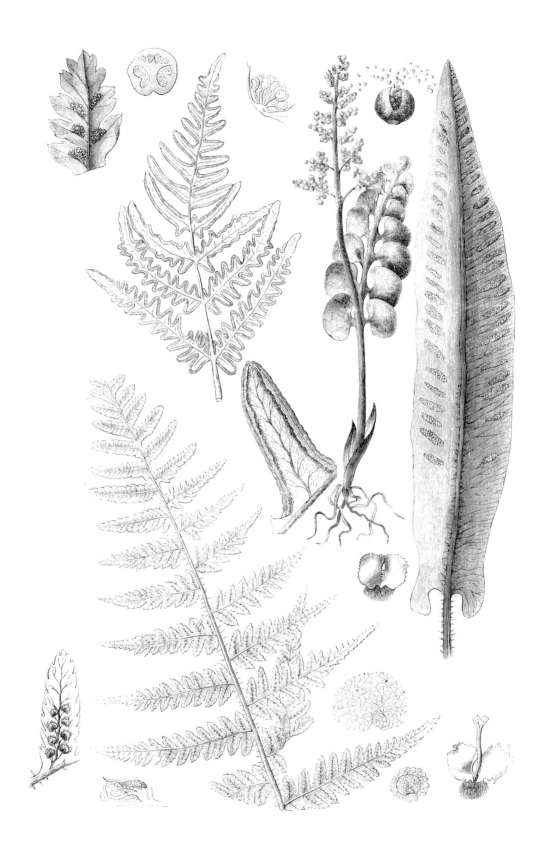

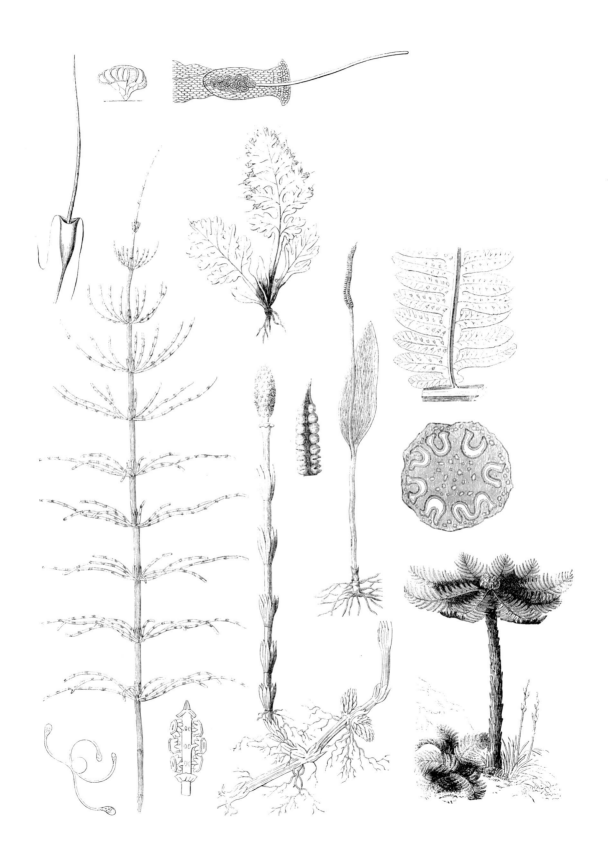

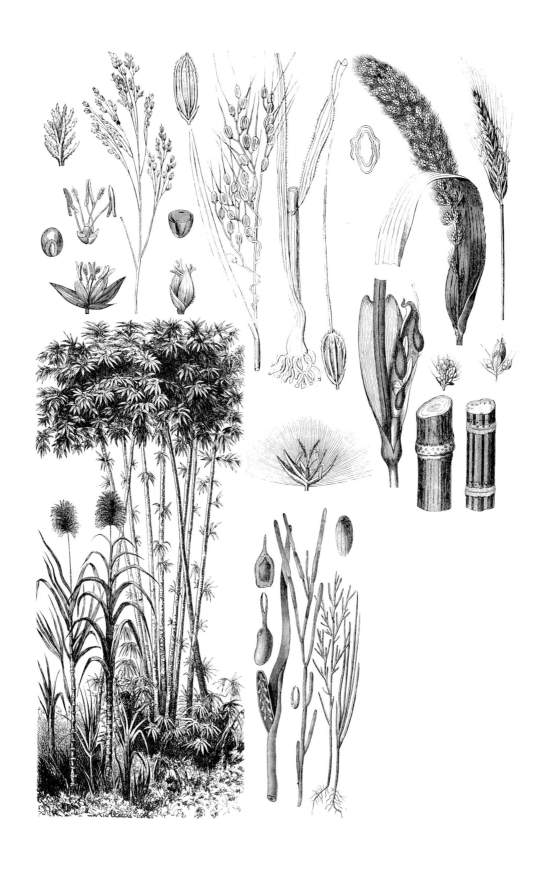

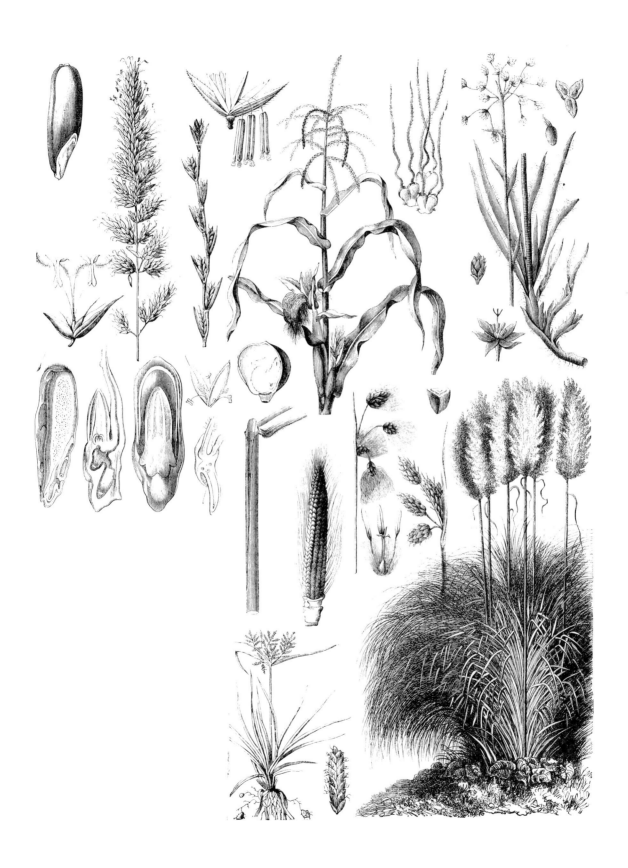

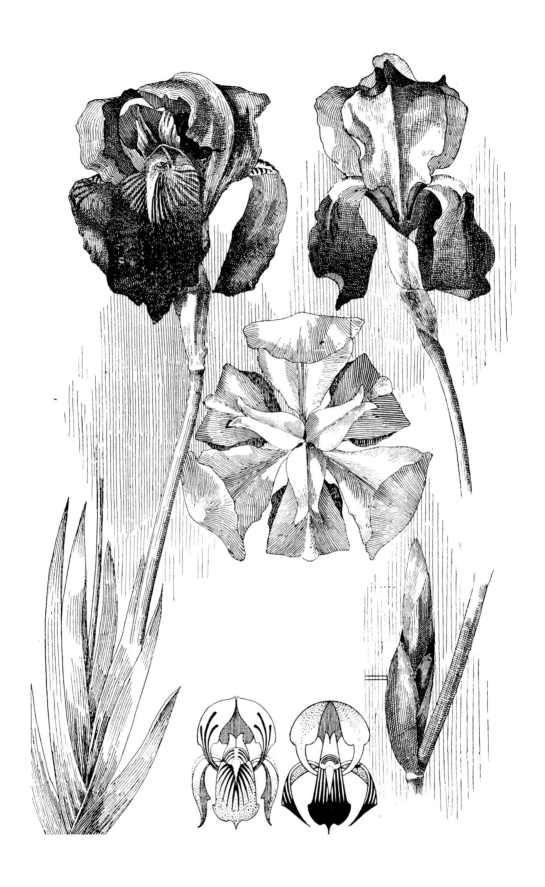

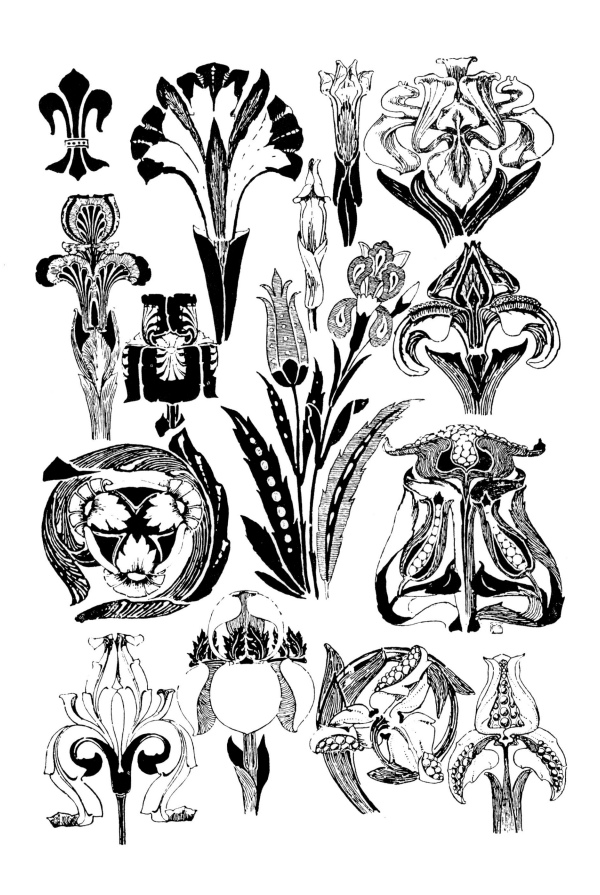

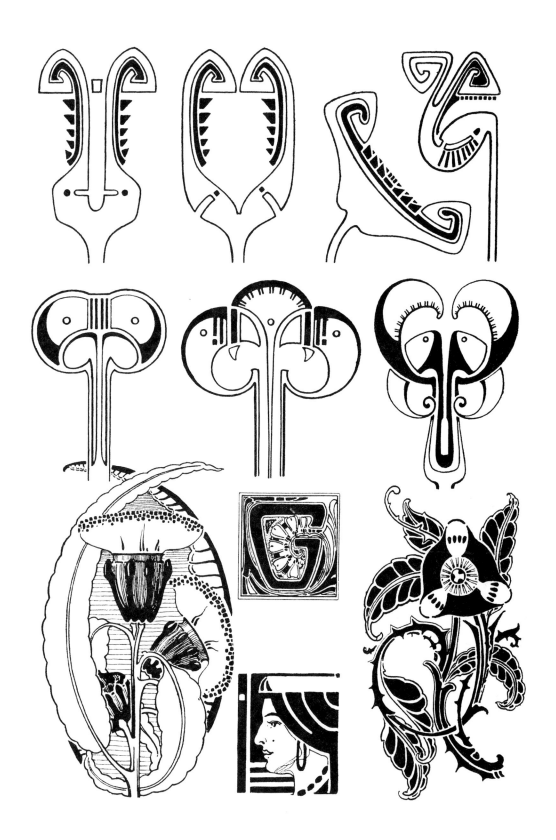

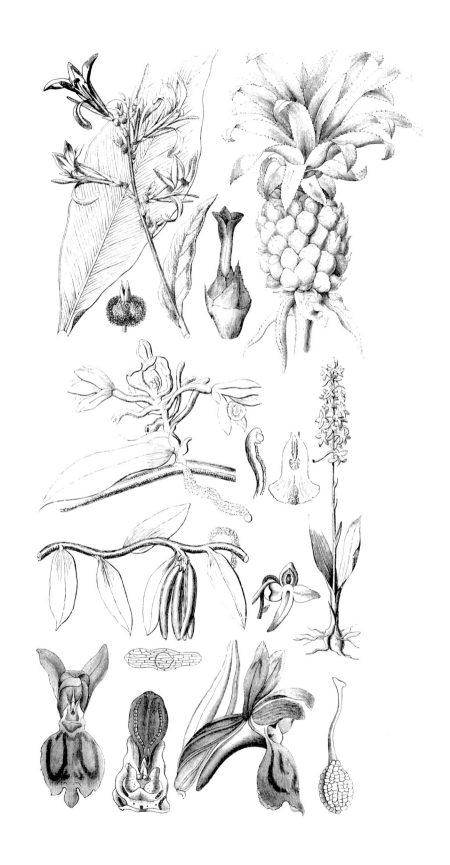

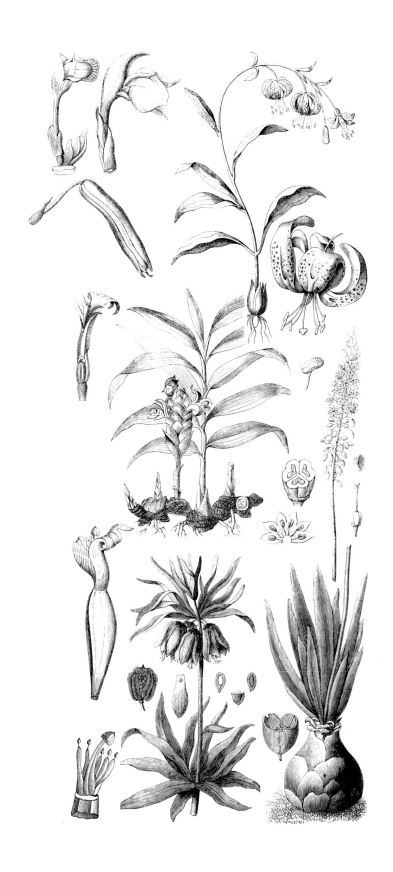

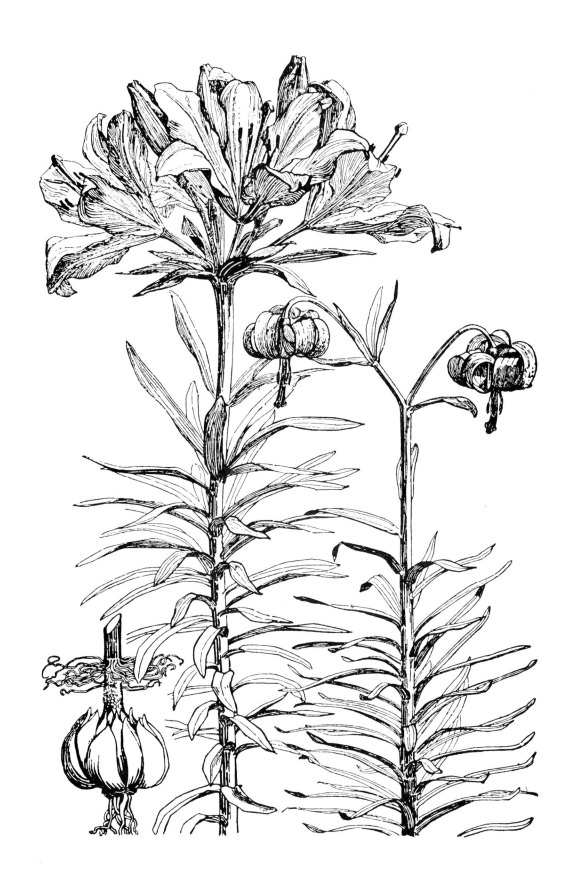

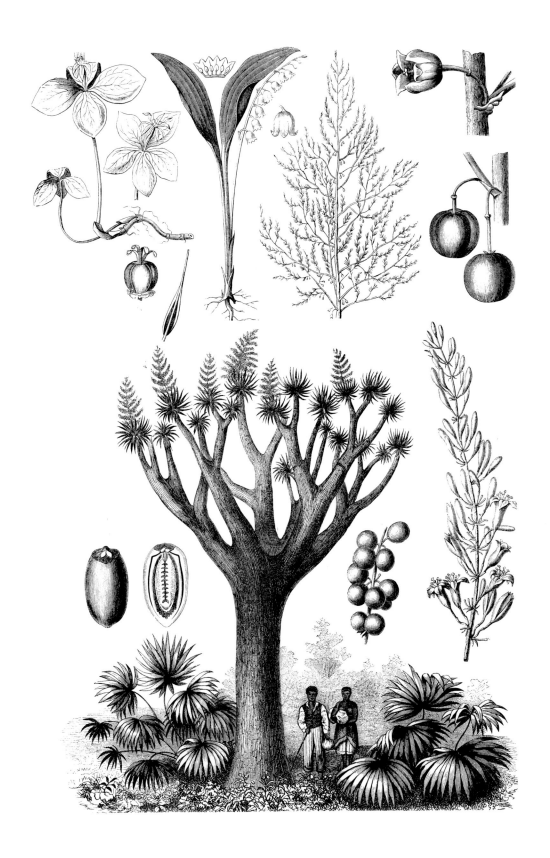

94

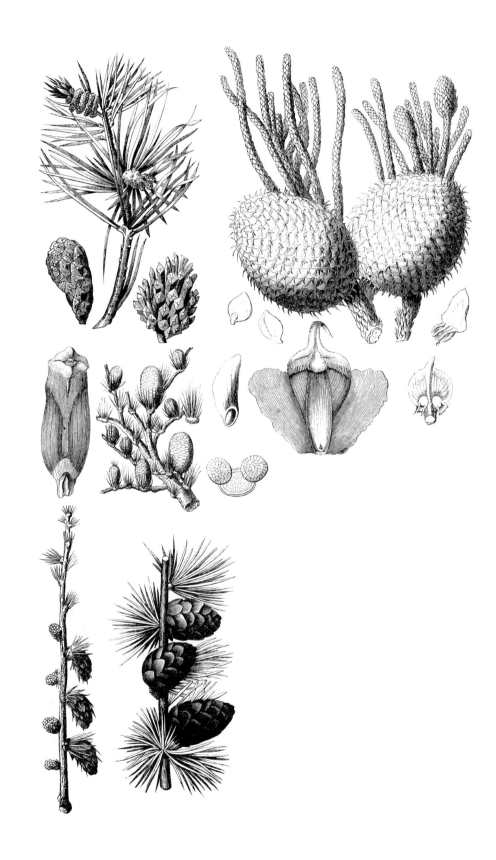

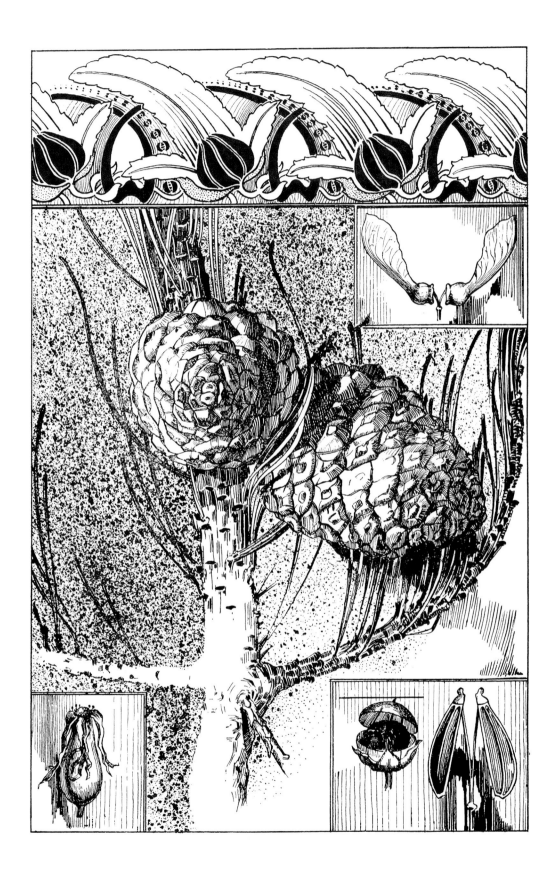

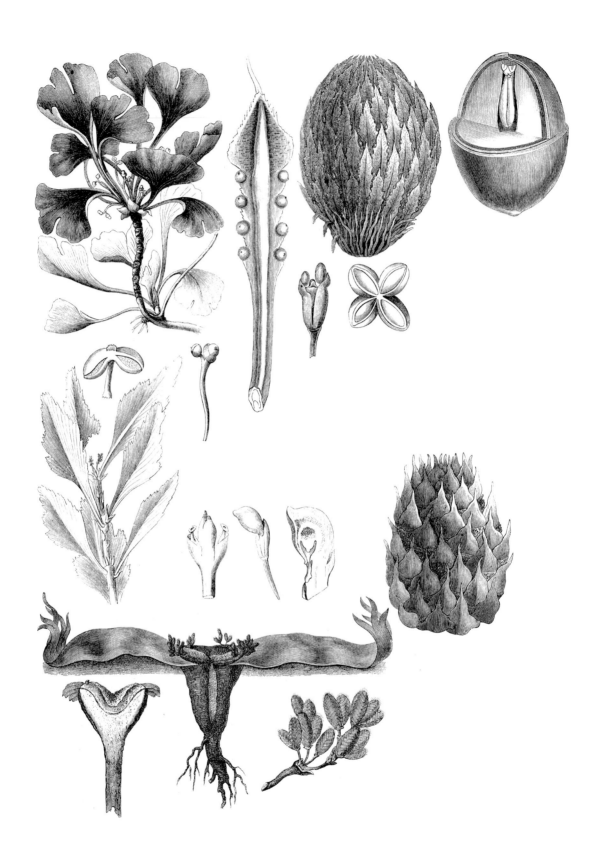

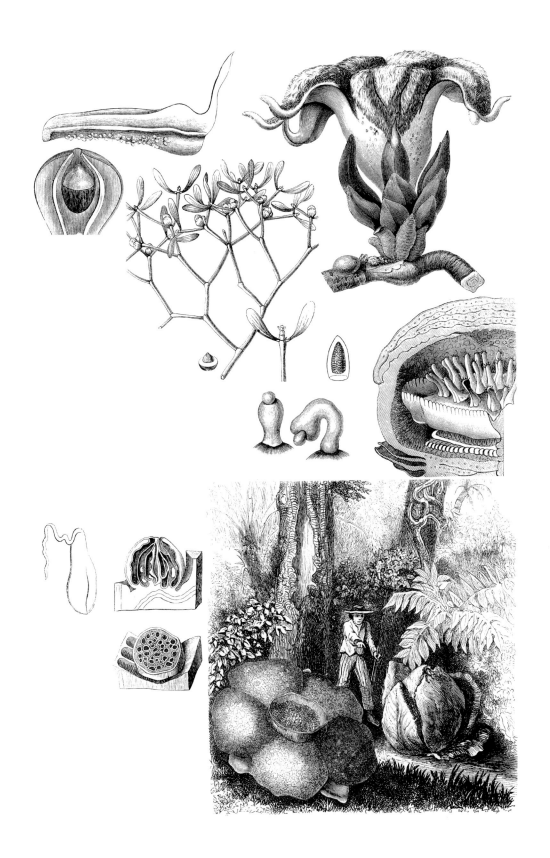

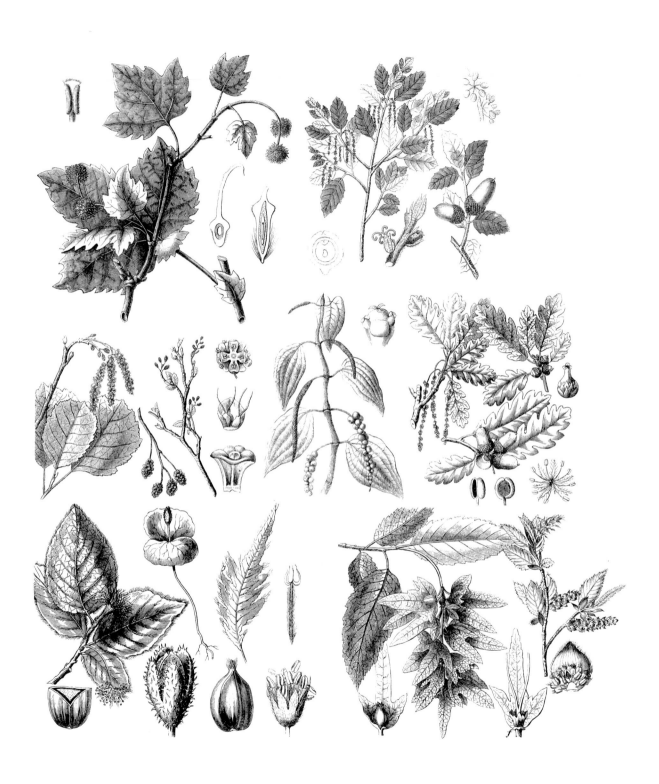

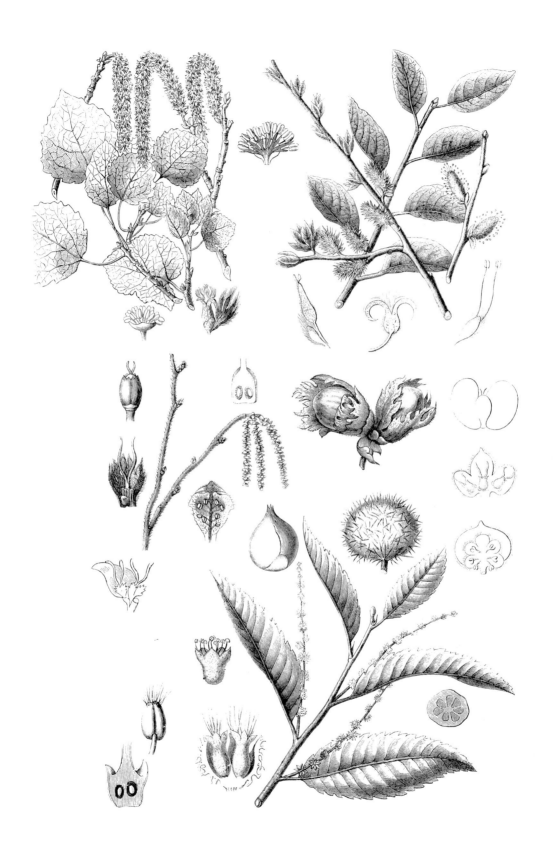

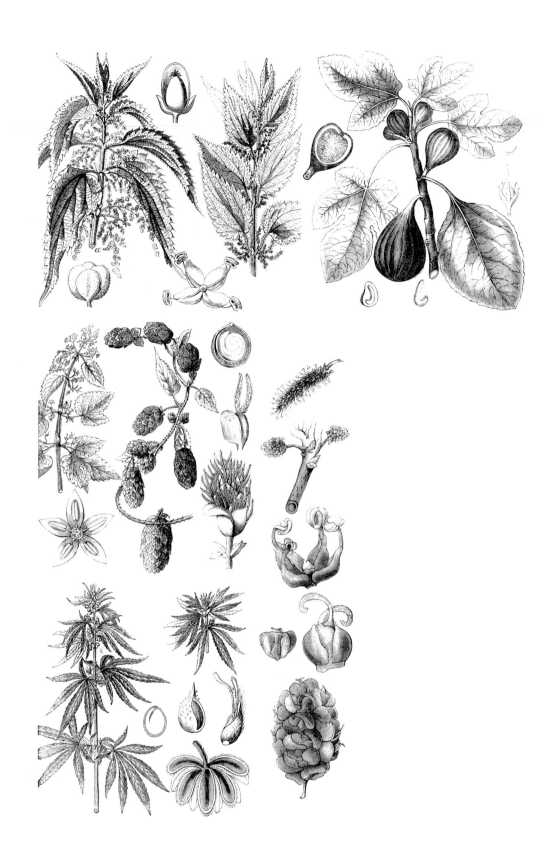

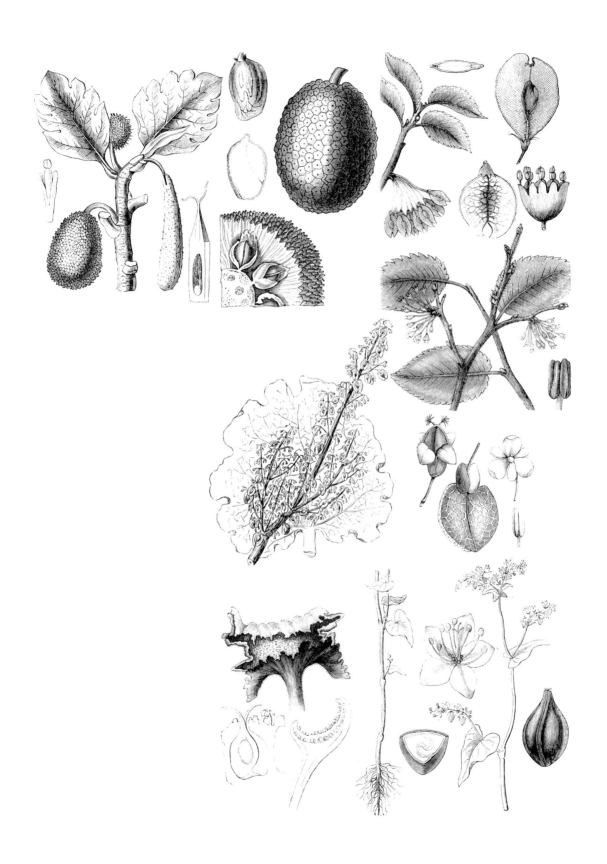

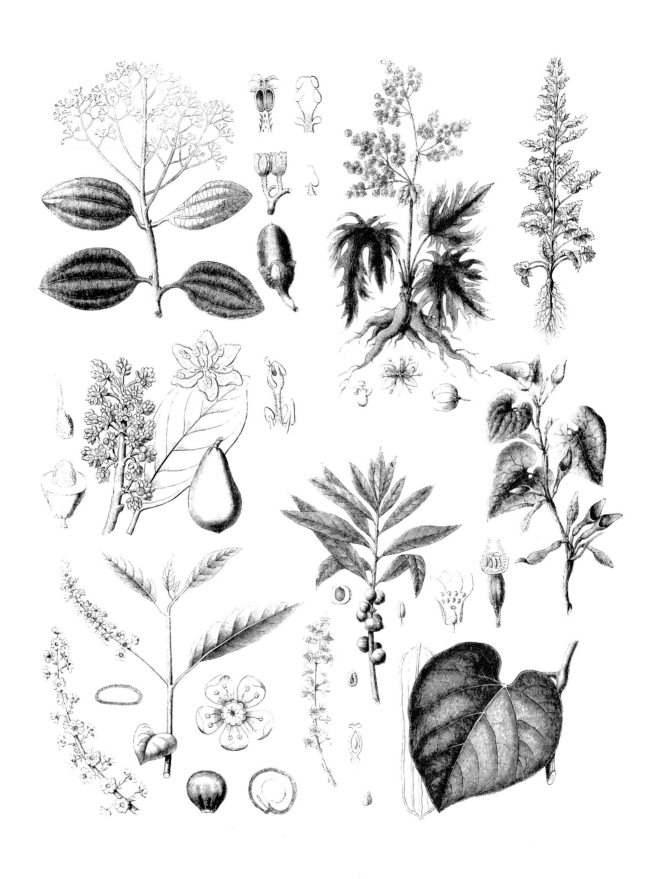

110

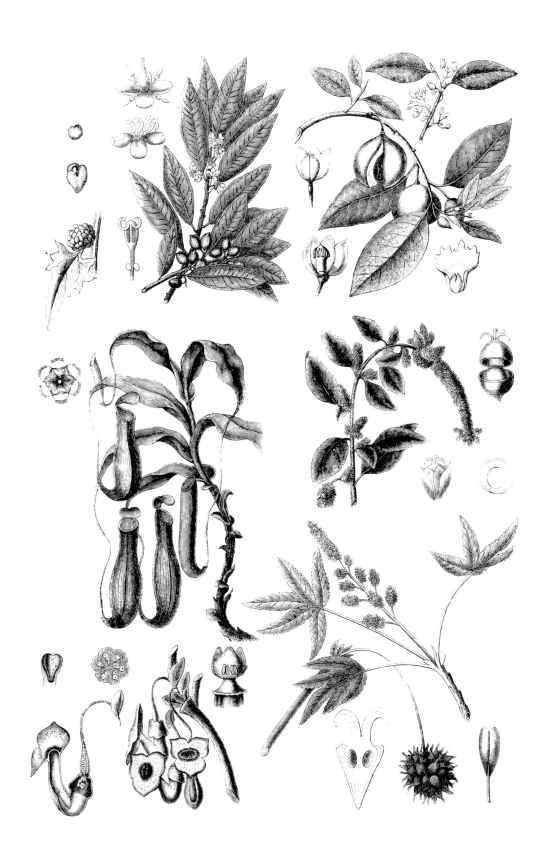

112

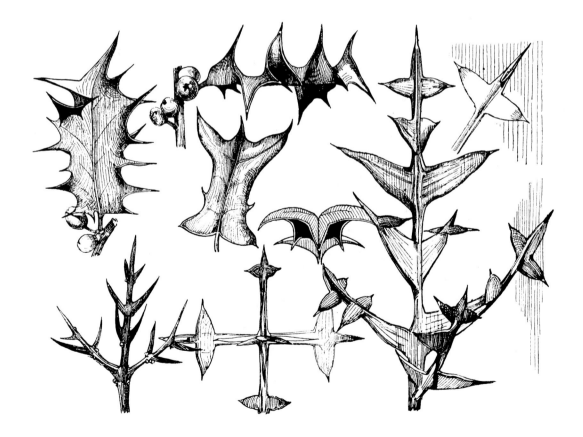

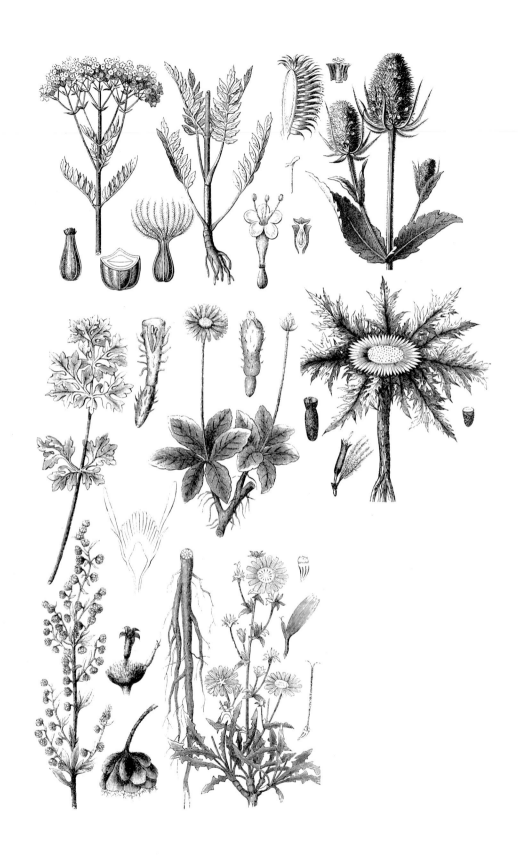

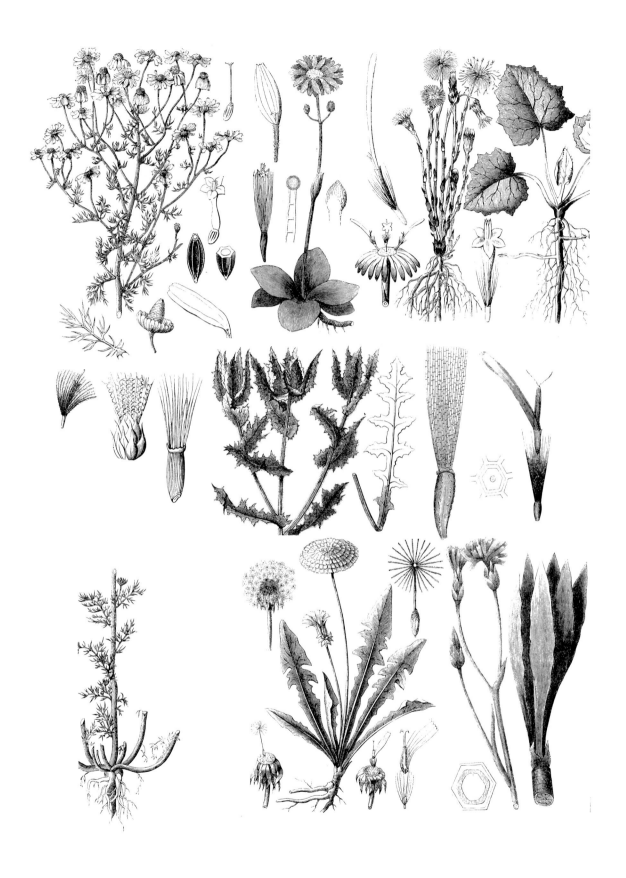

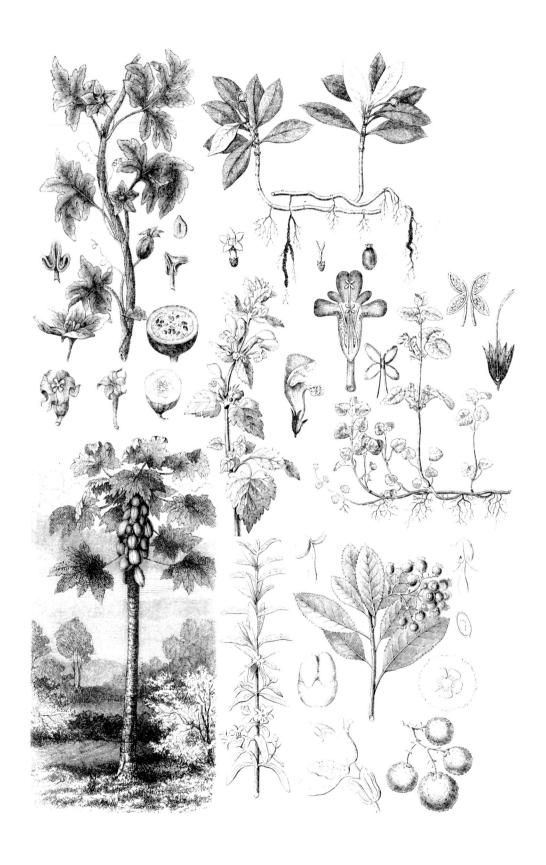

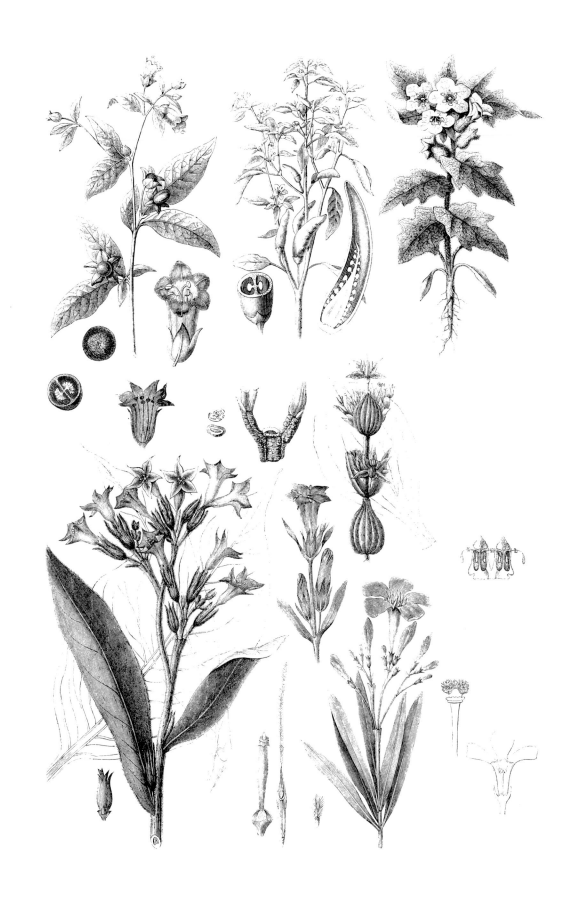

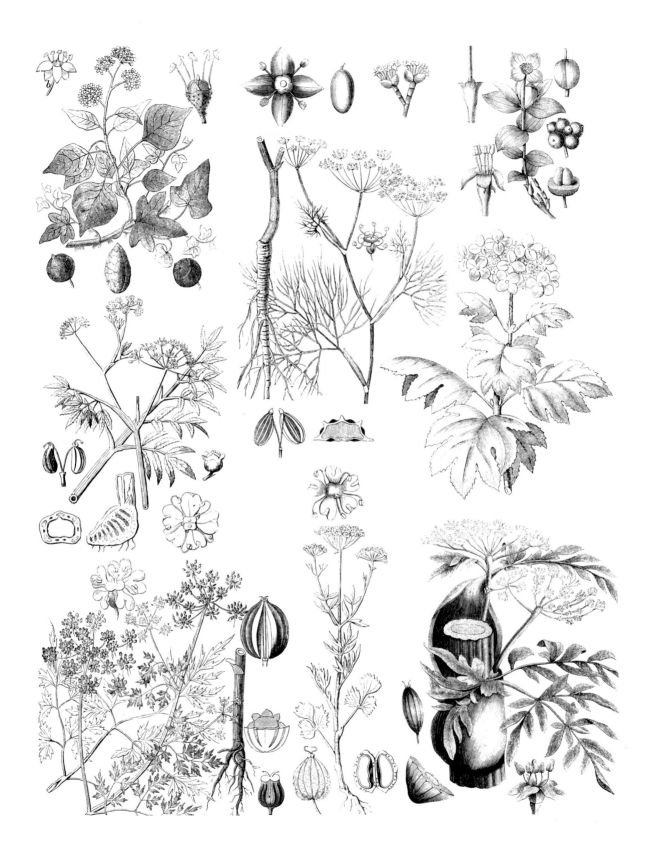

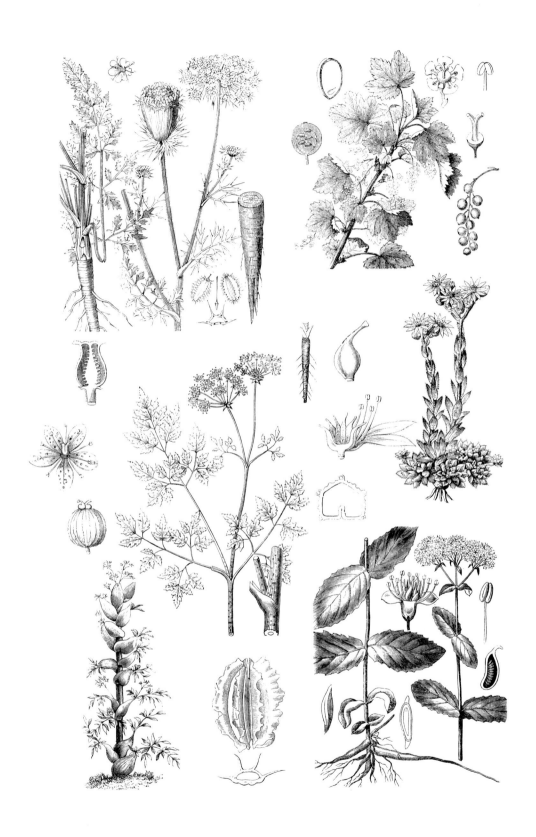

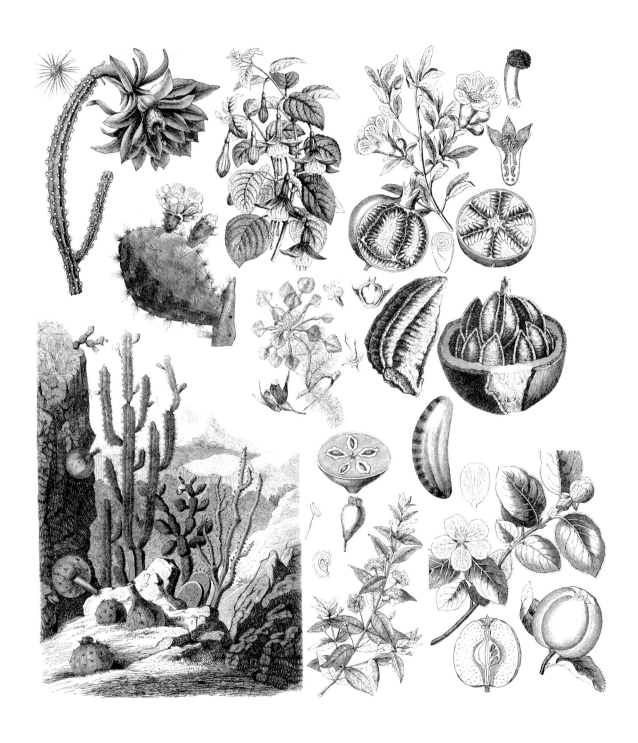

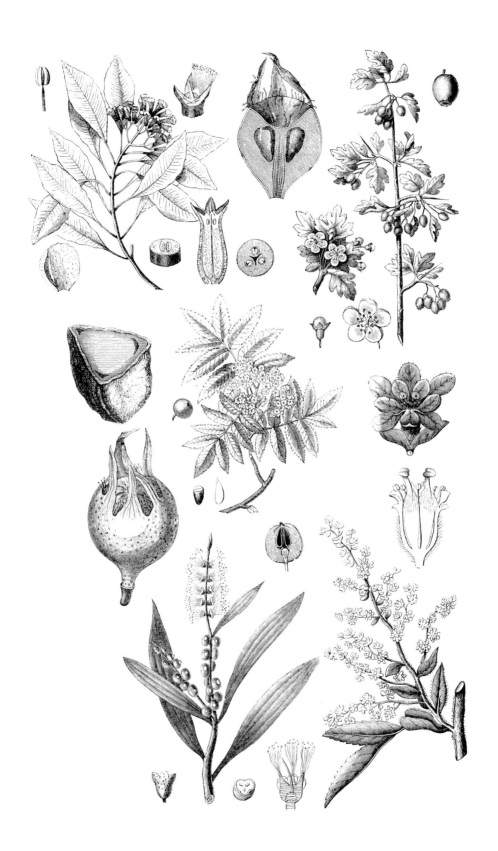

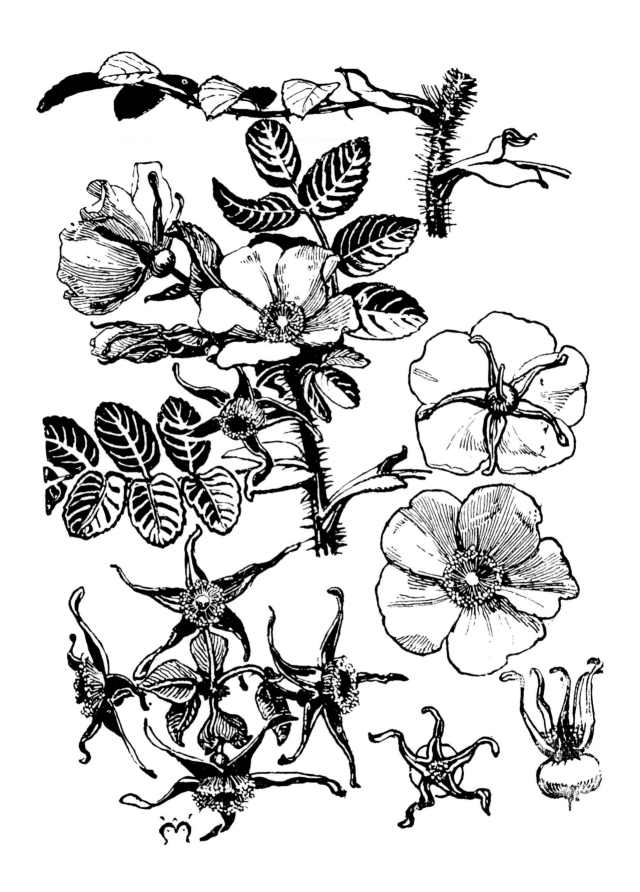

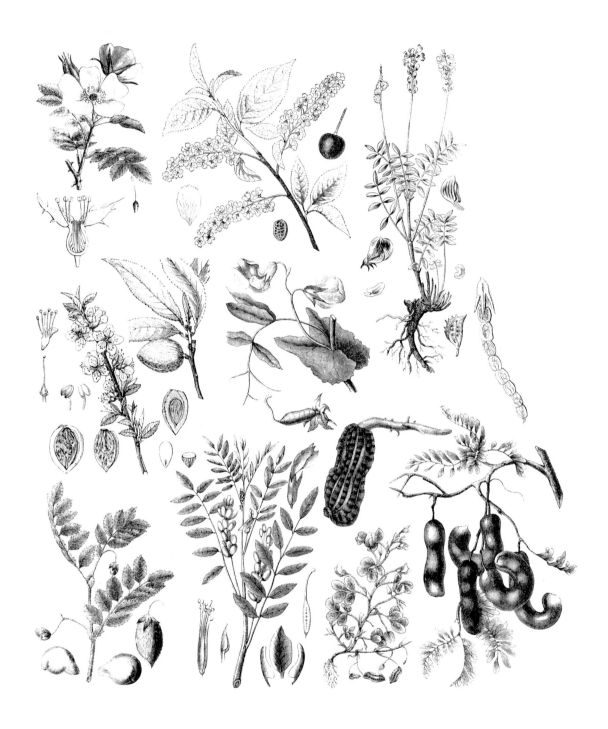

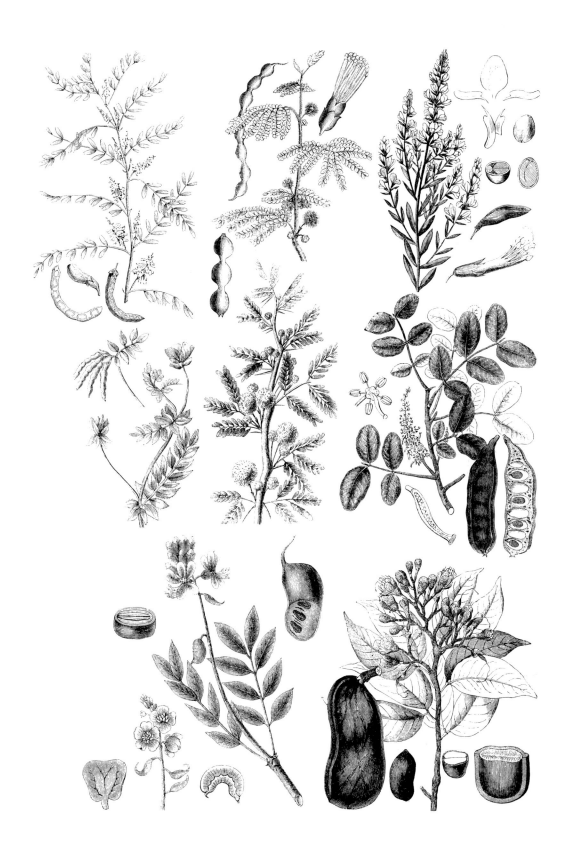

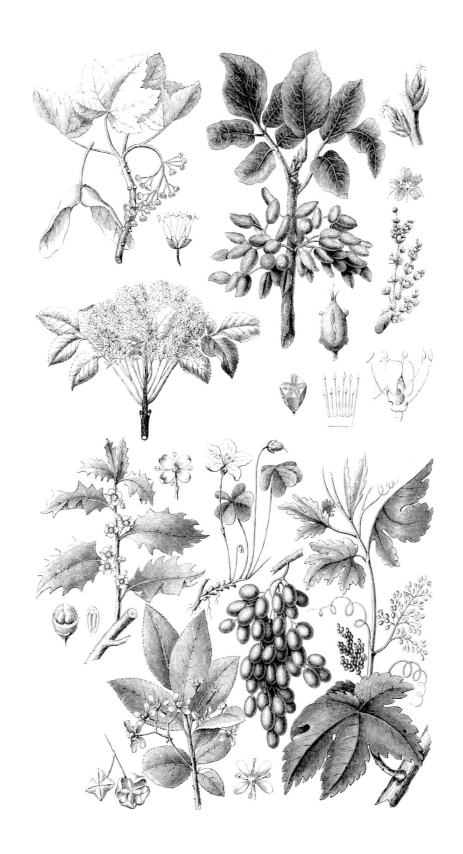

138

139

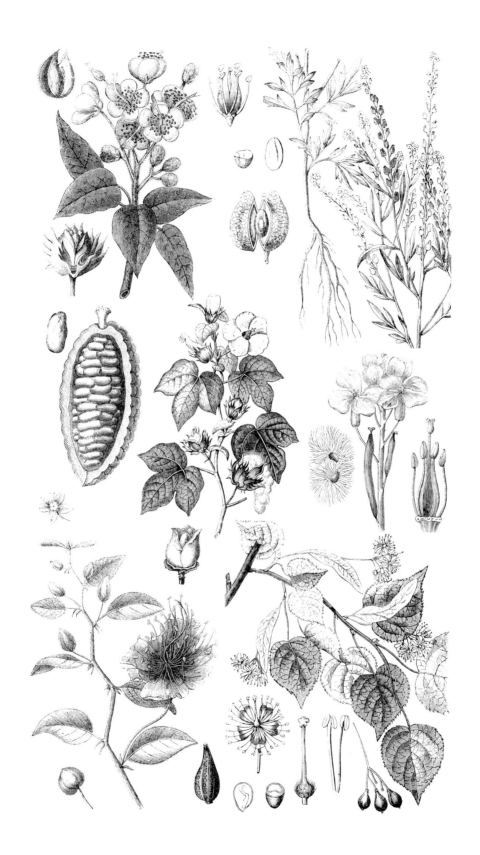

144

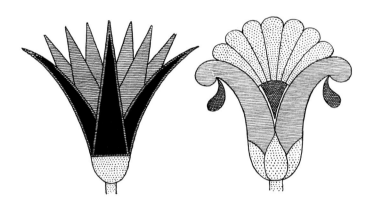

147

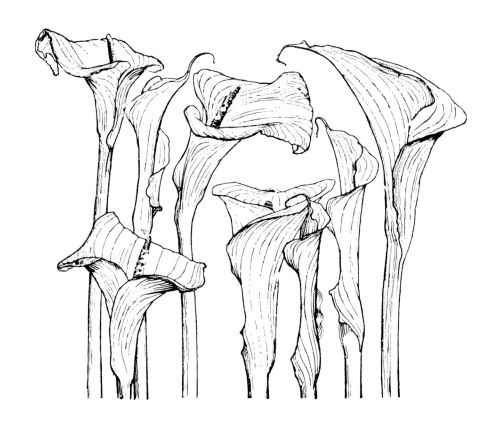

150

151

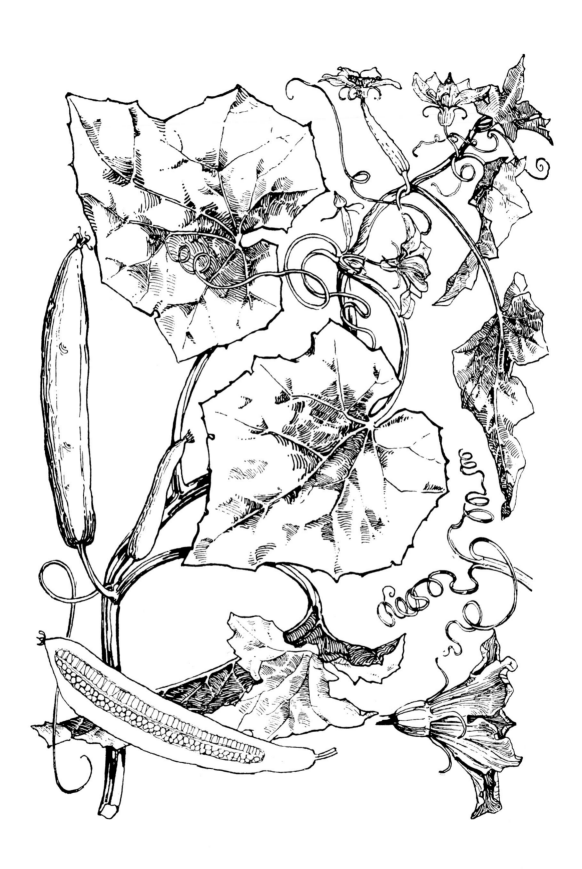

152

154

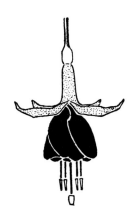

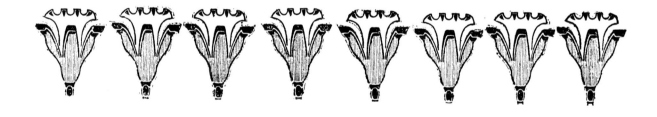

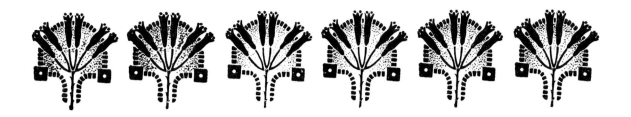

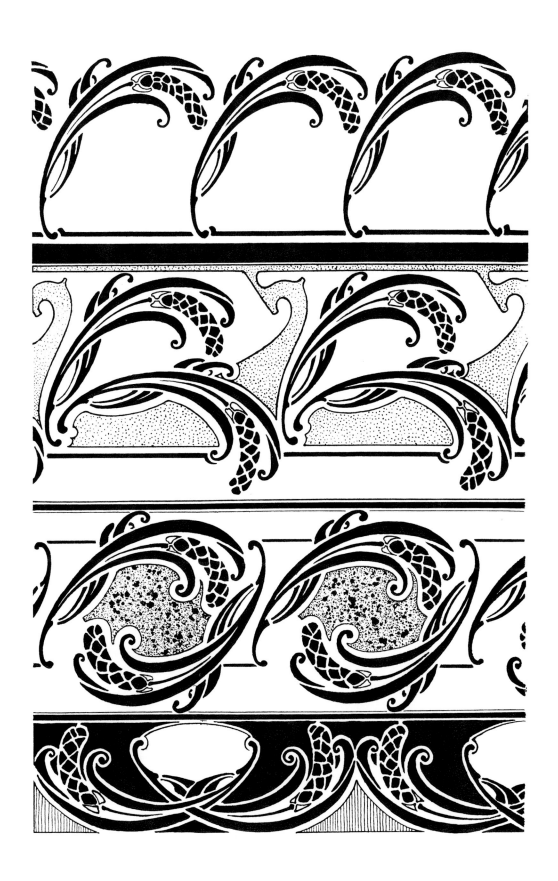

159

164

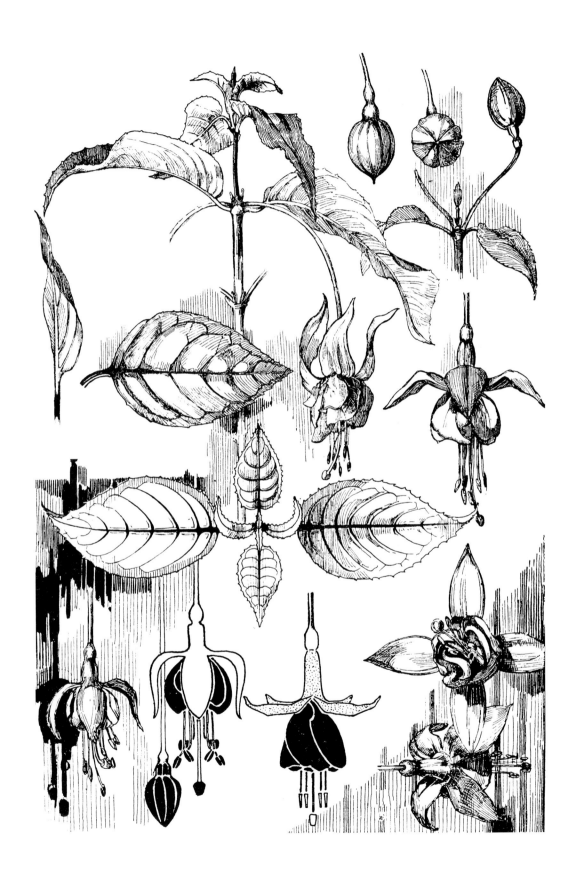

166

169

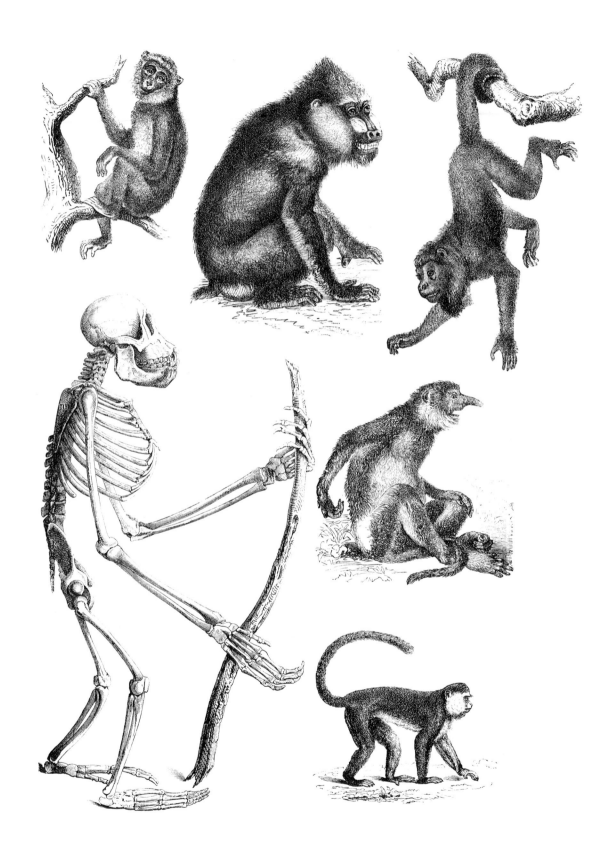

172

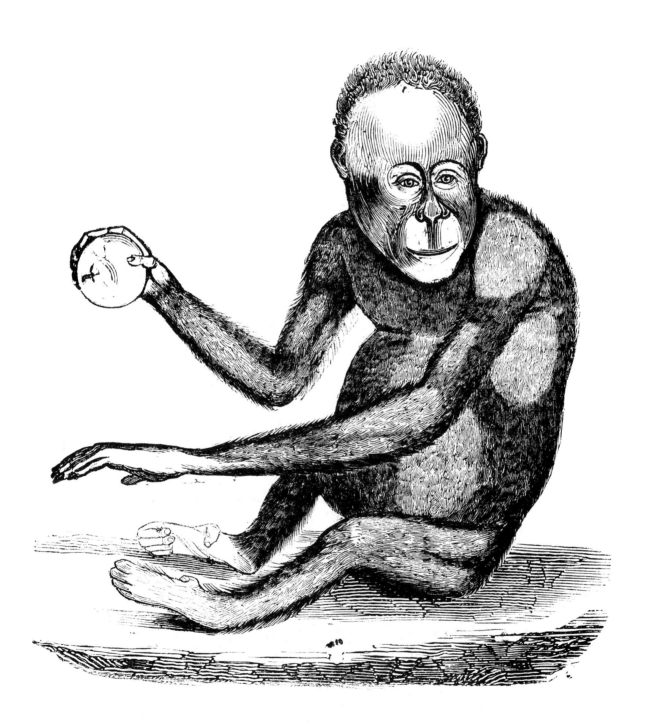

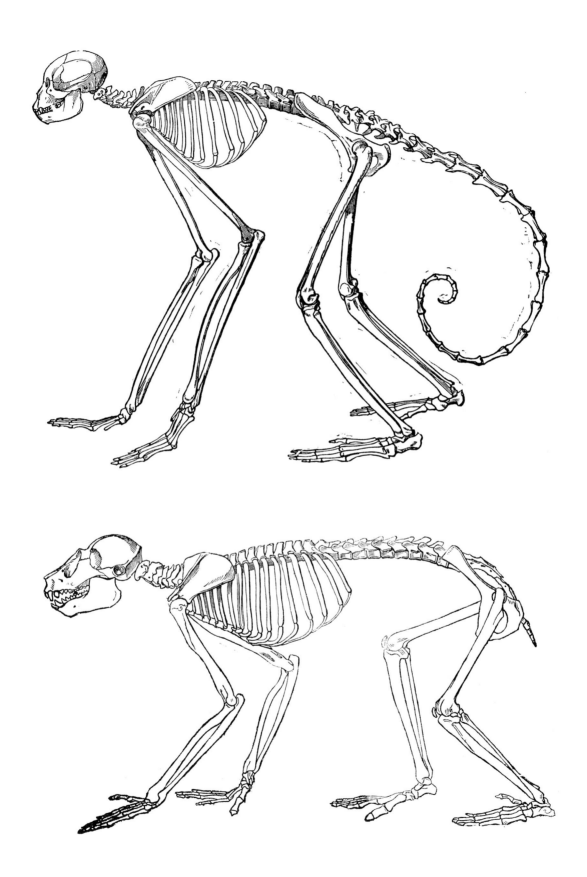

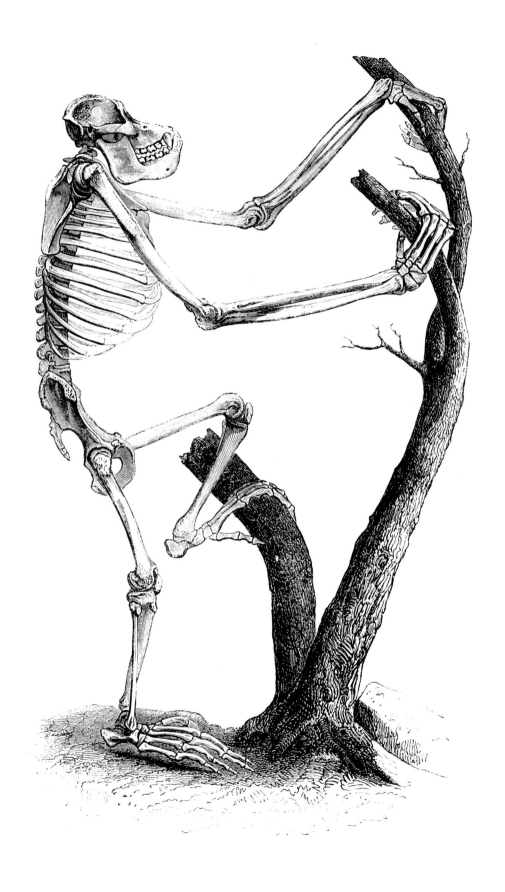

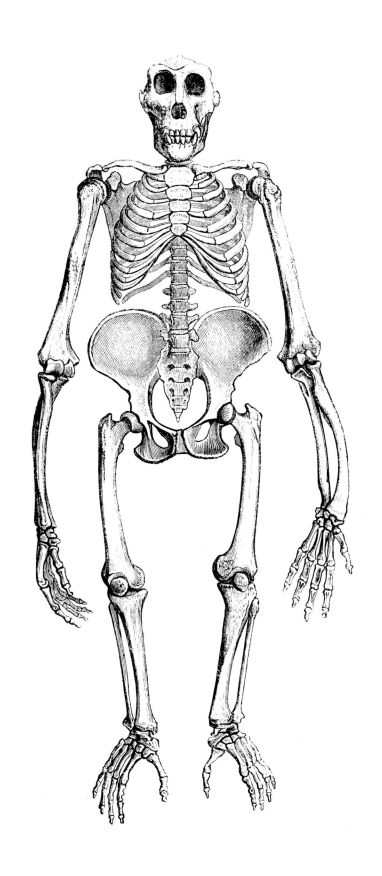

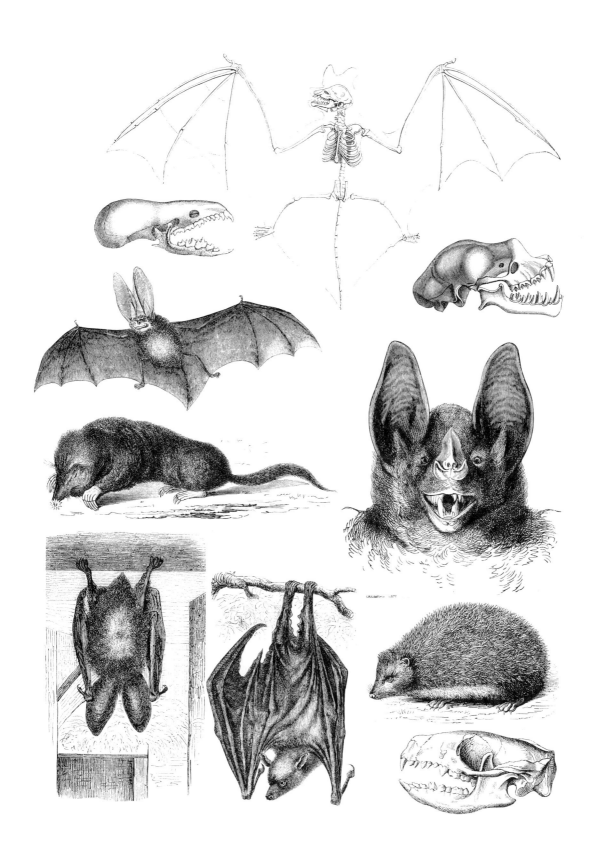

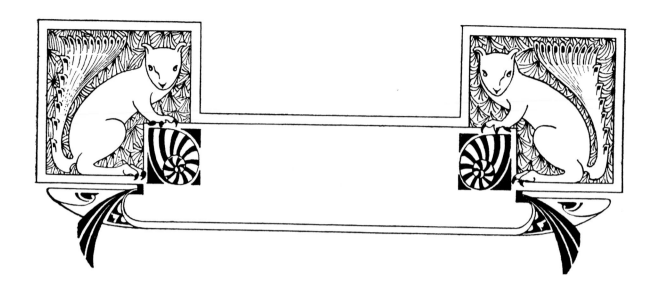

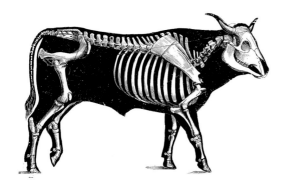

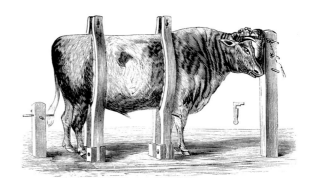

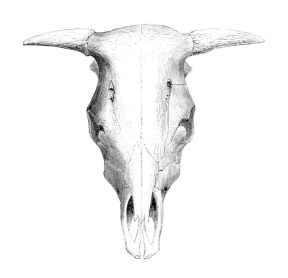

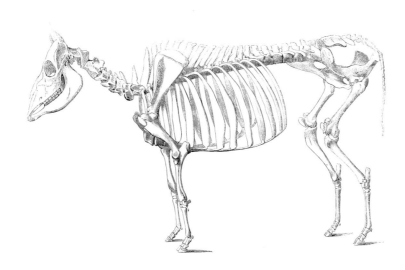

215

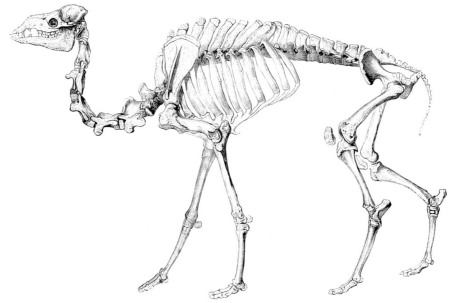

219

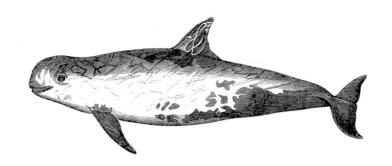

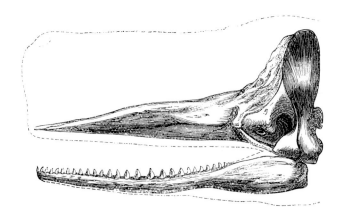

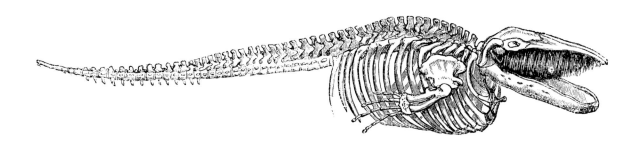

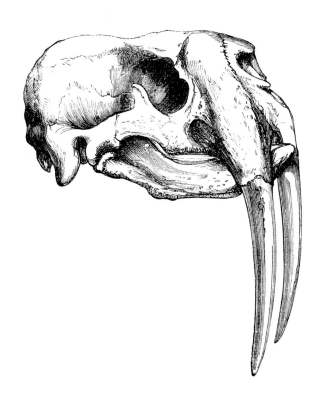

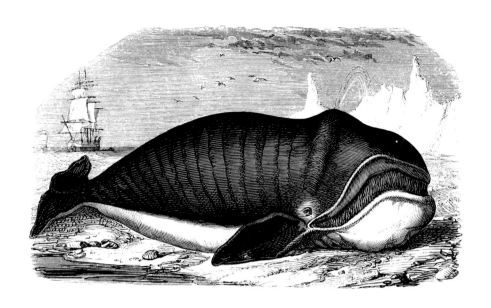

237

239

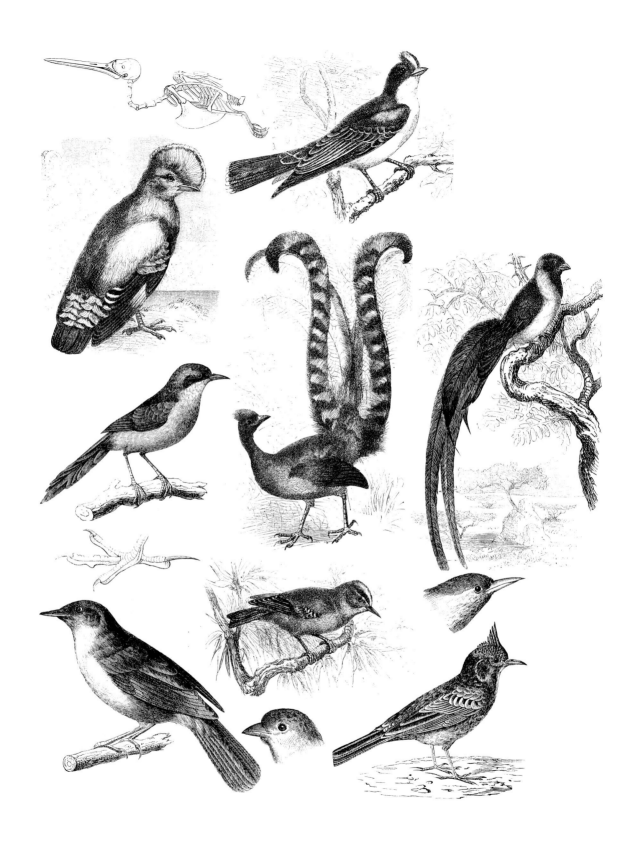

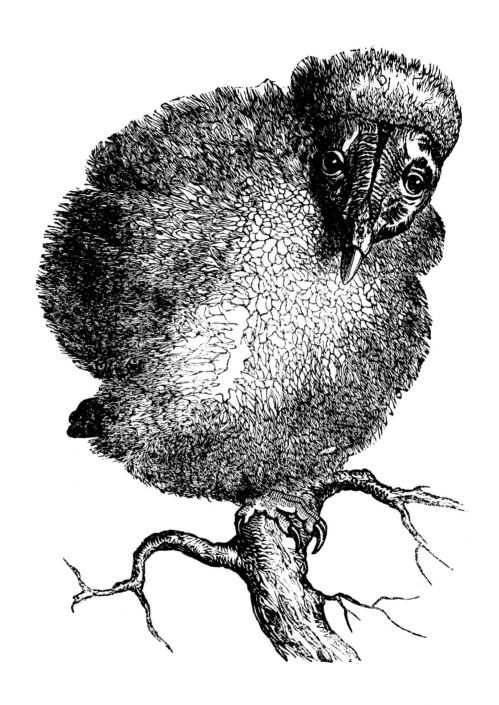

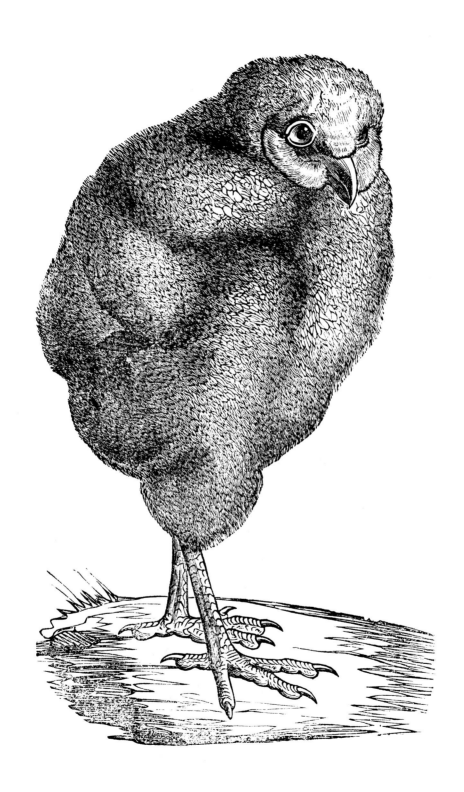

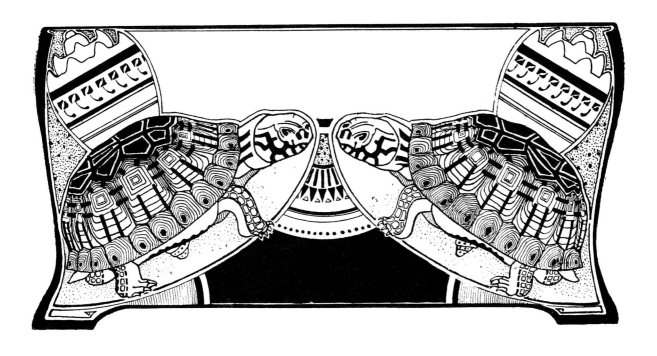

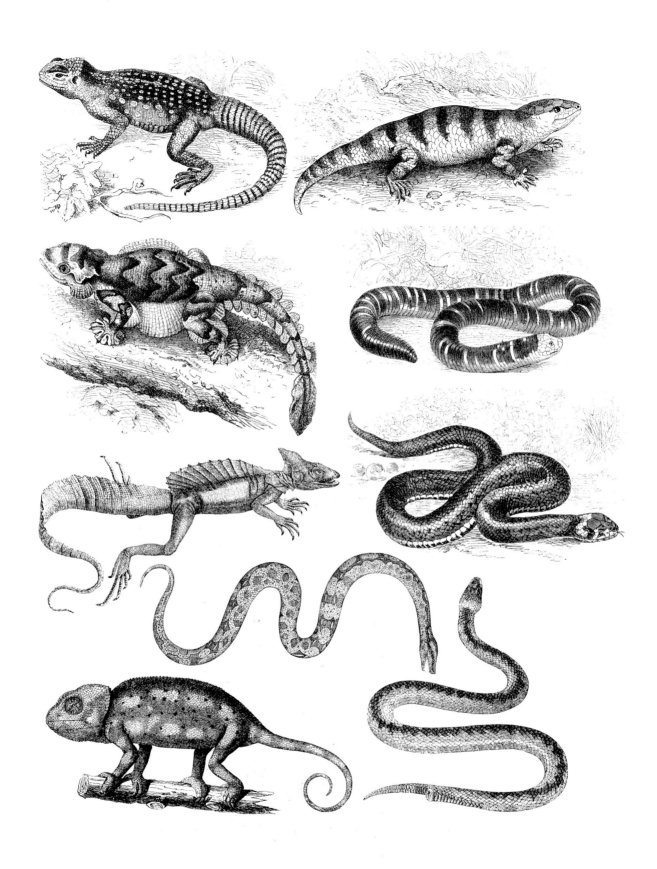

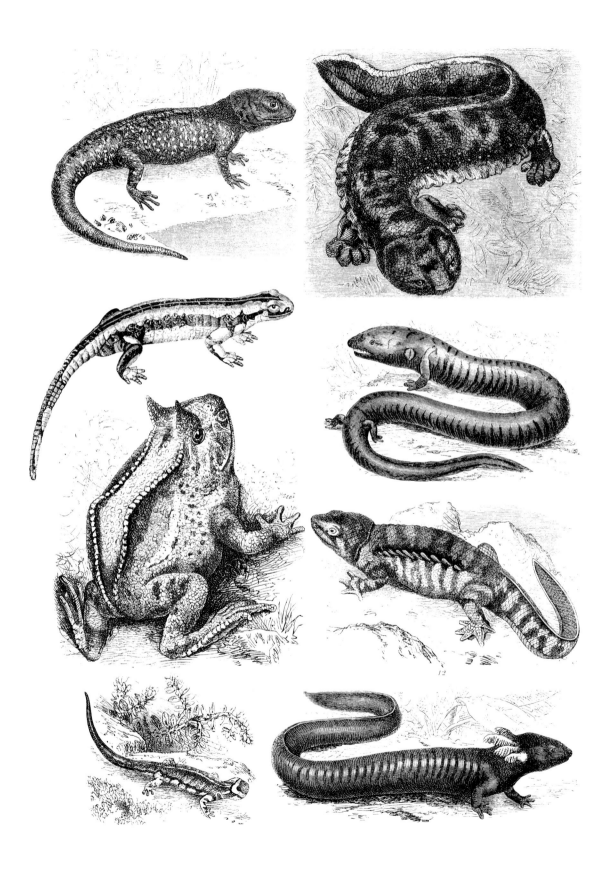

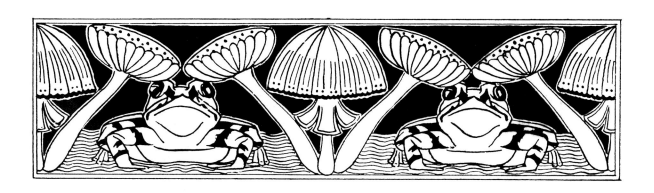

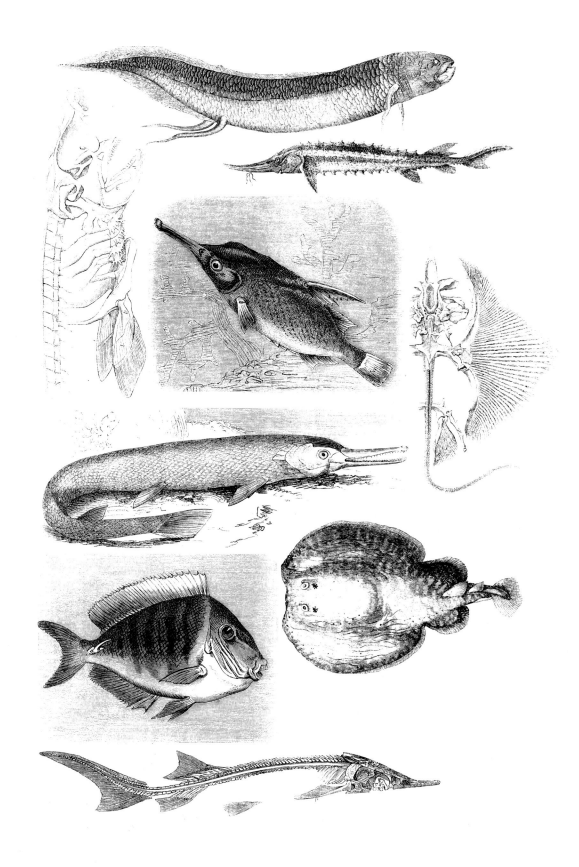

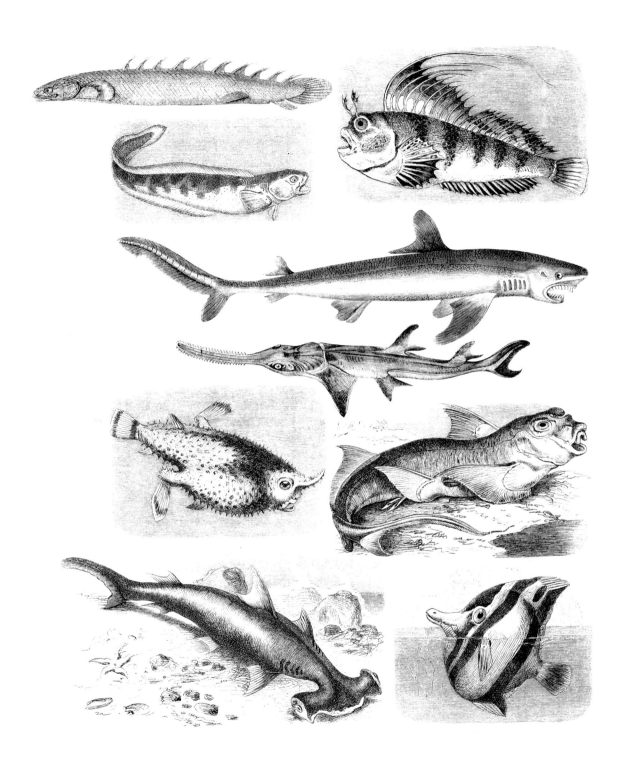

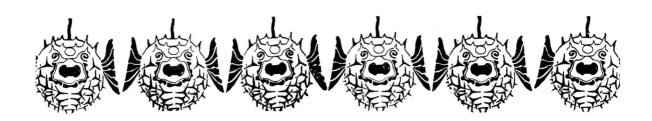

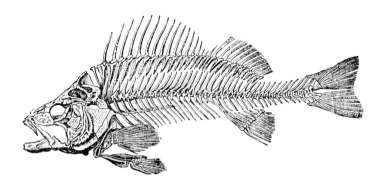

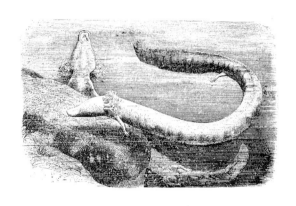

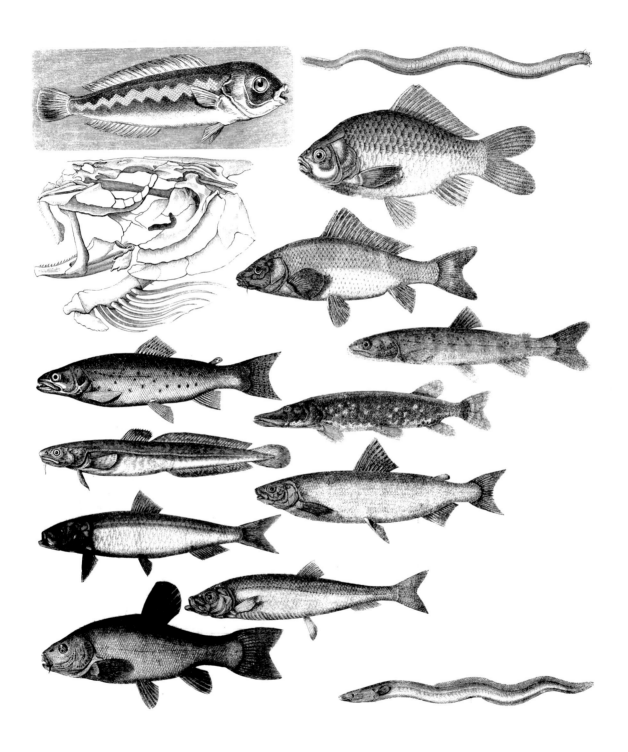

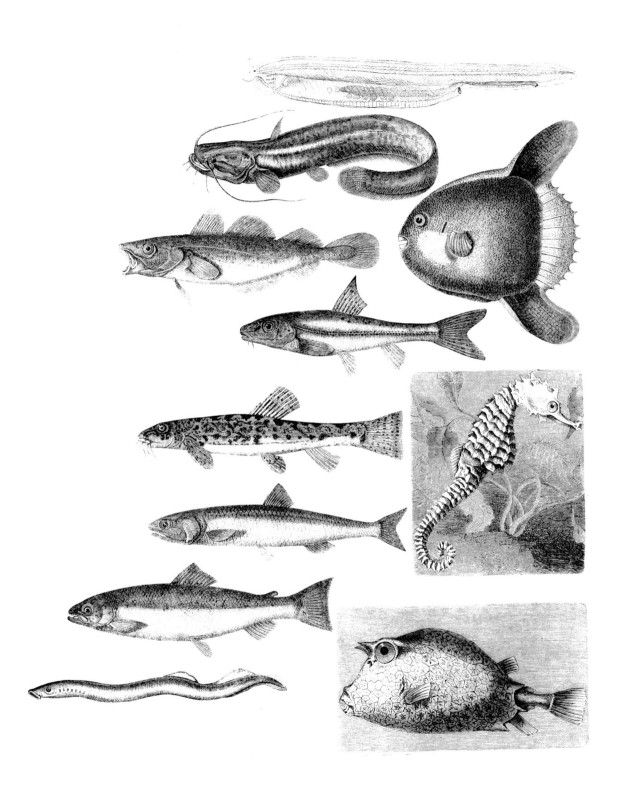

299

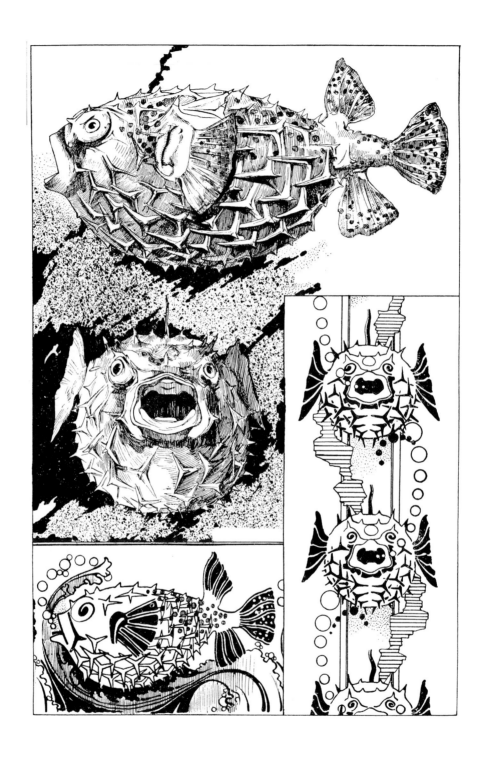

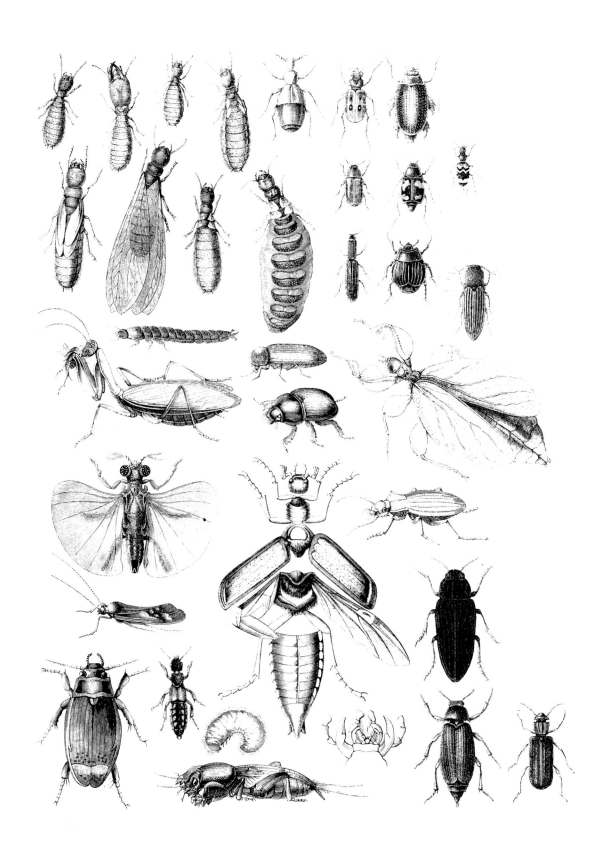

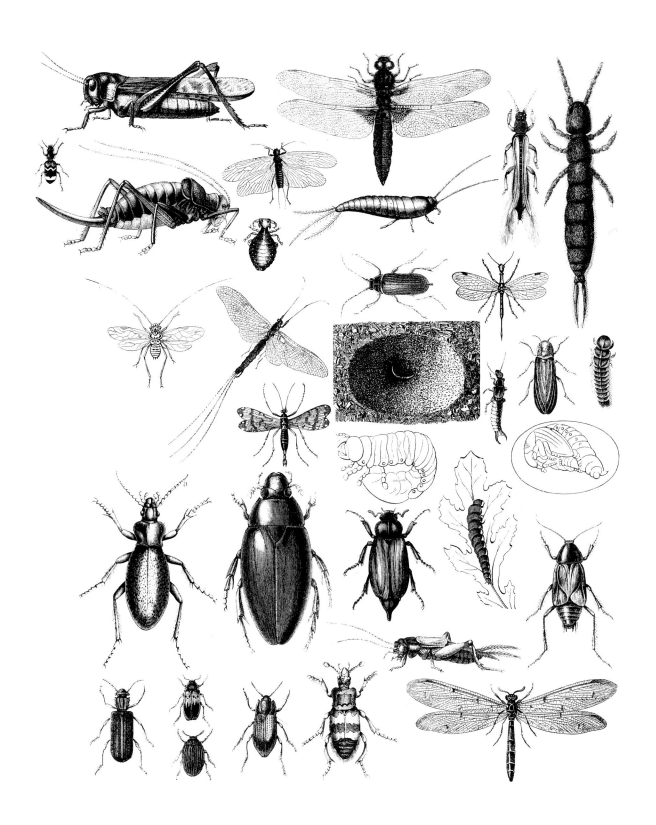

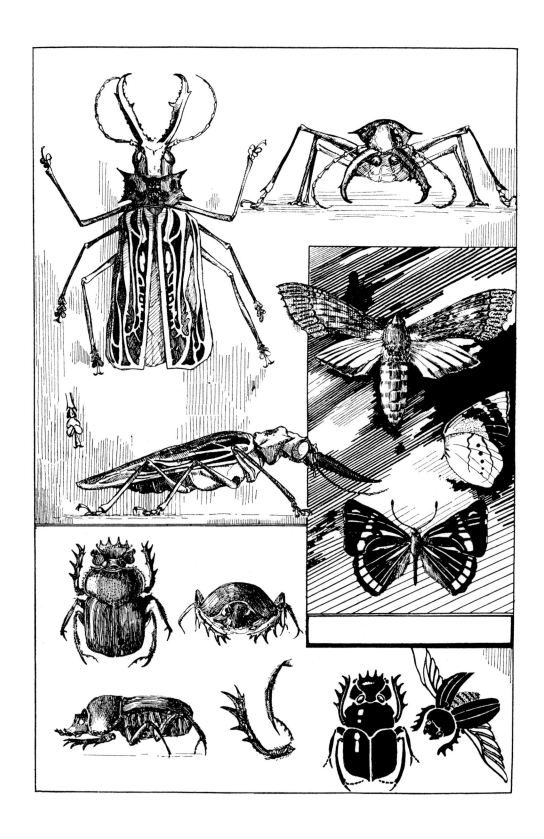

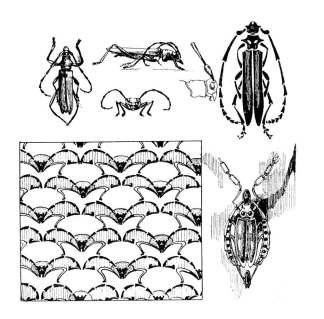

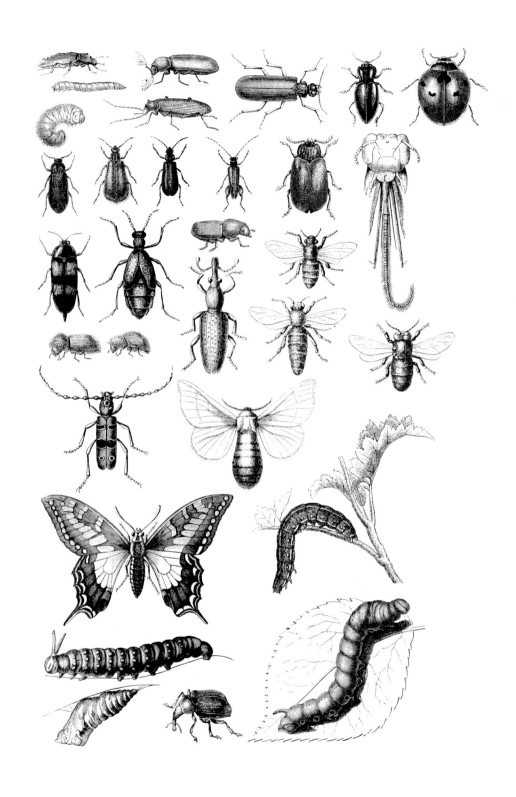

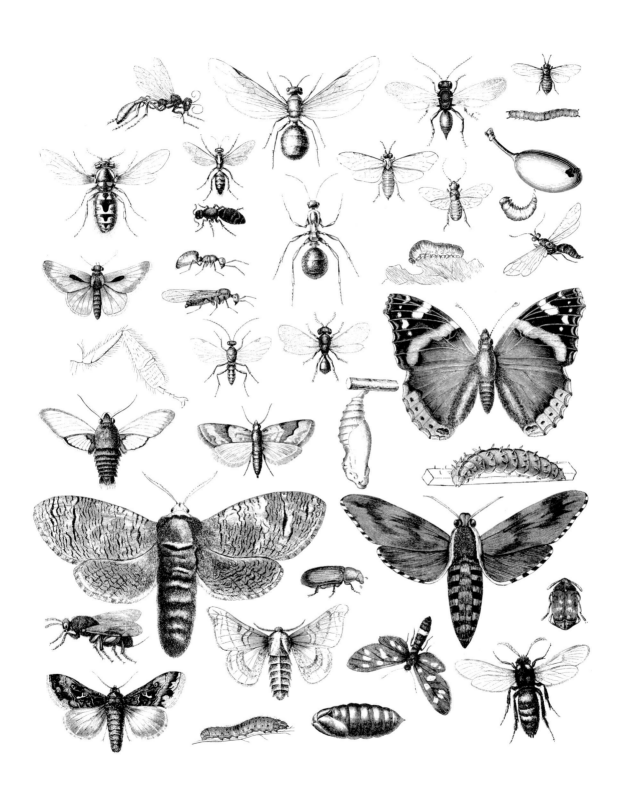

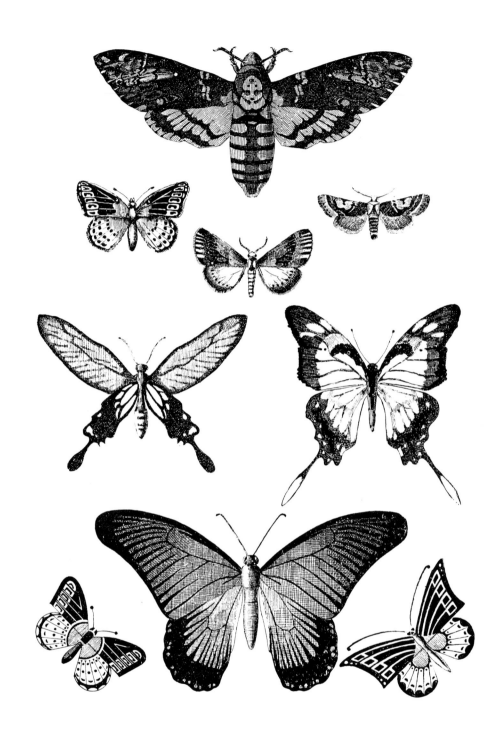

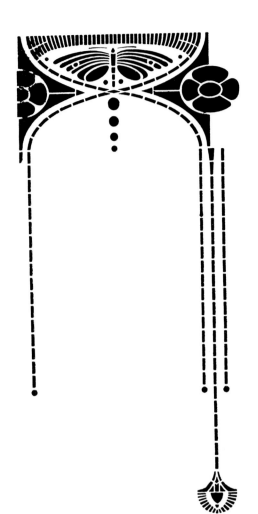

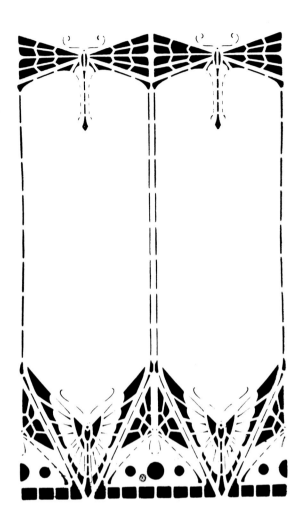

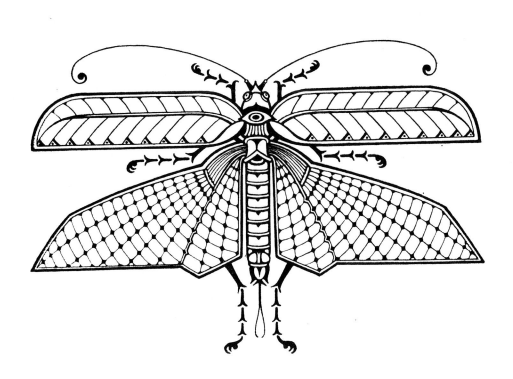

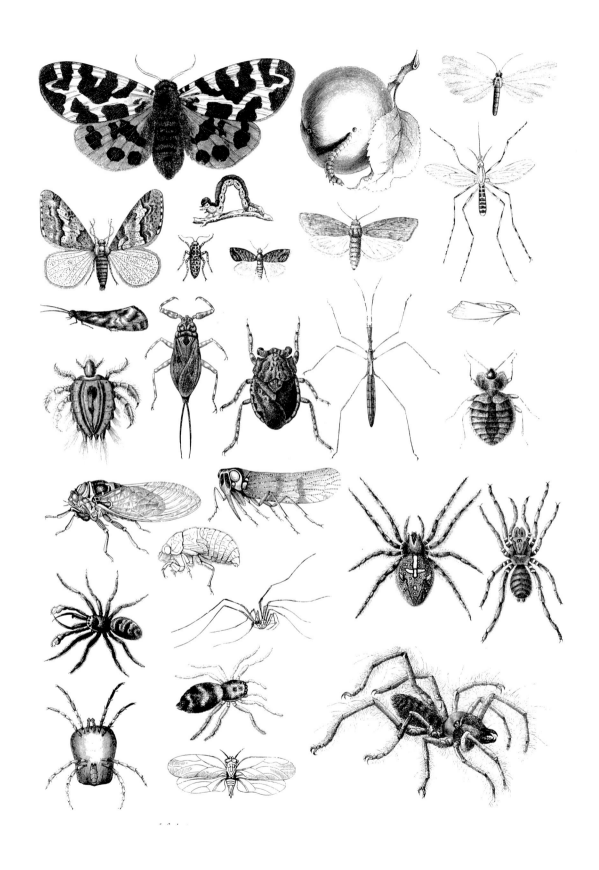

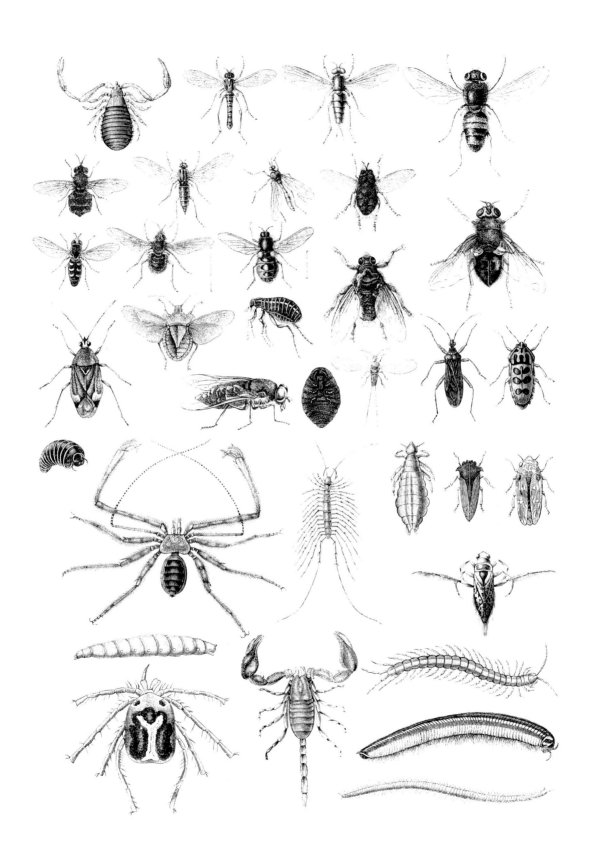

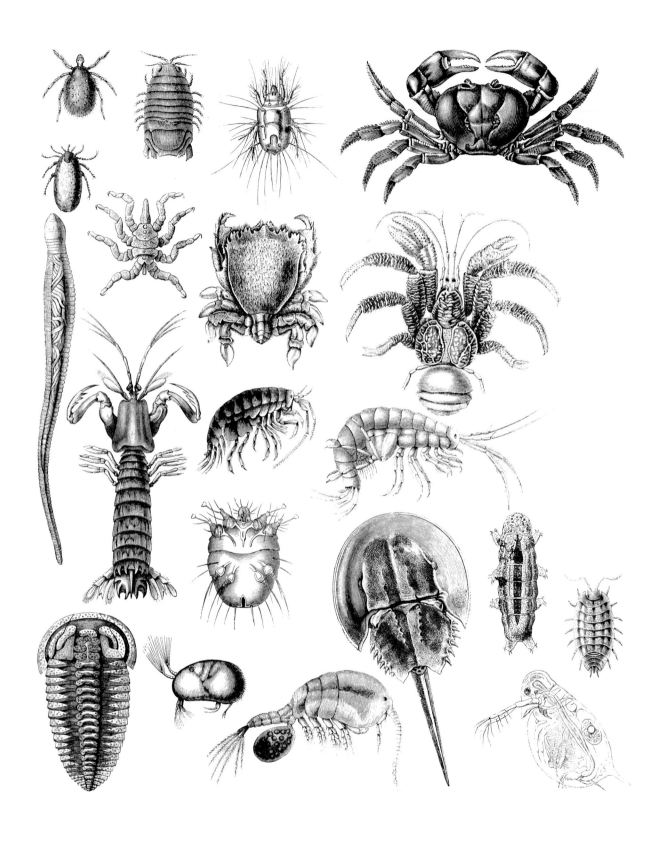

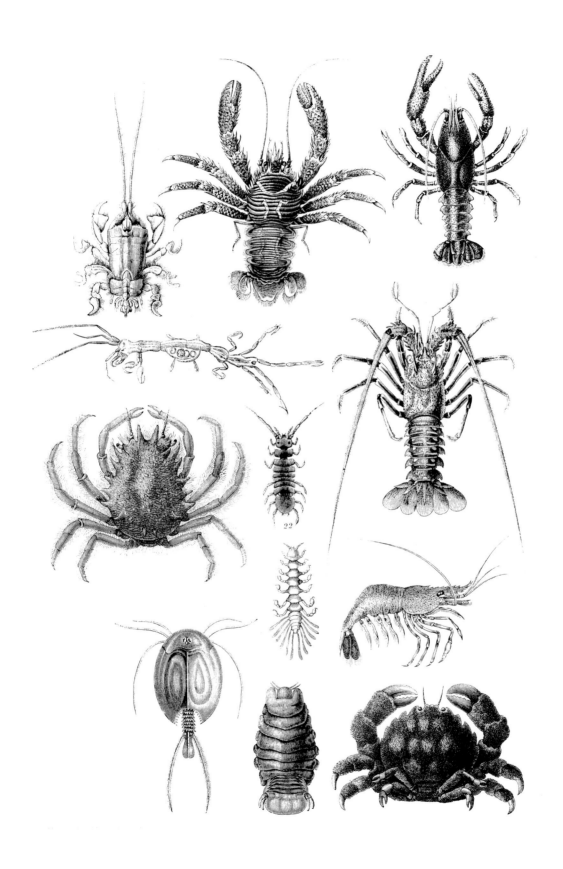

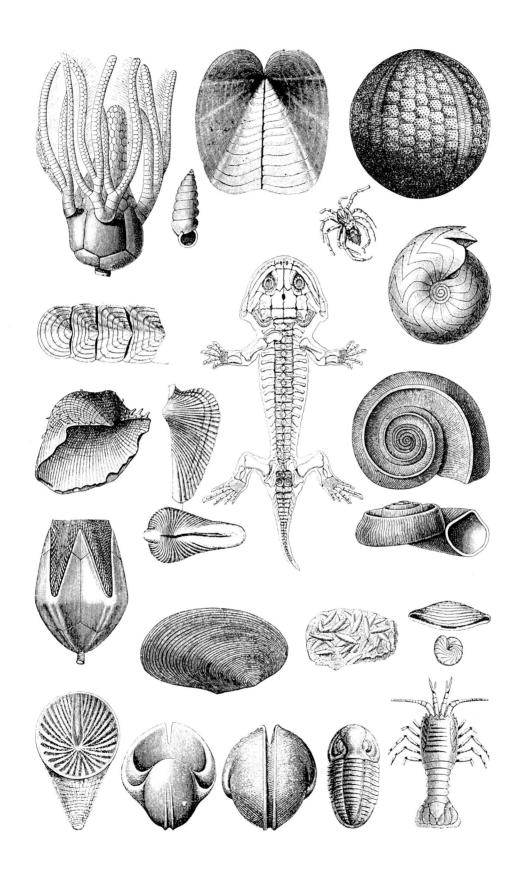

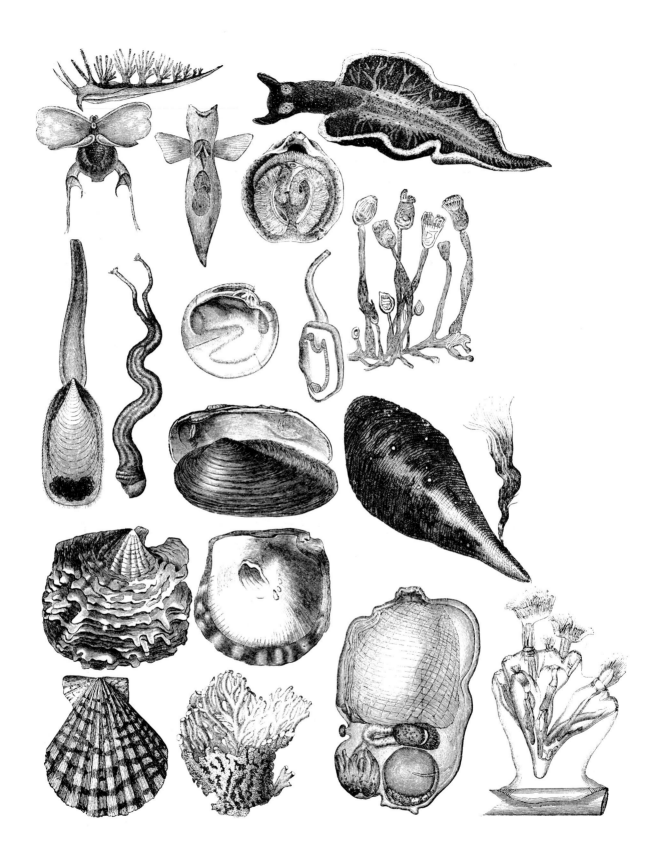

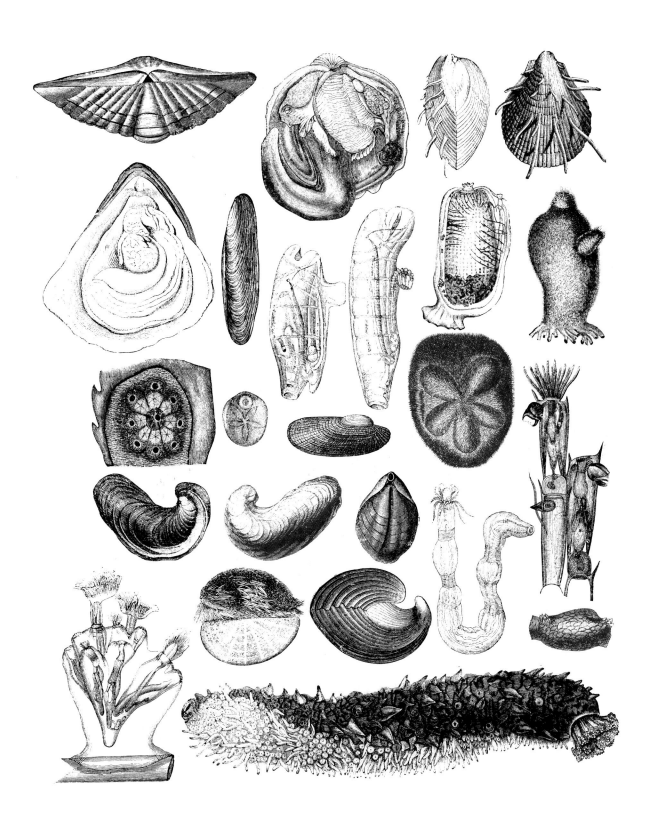

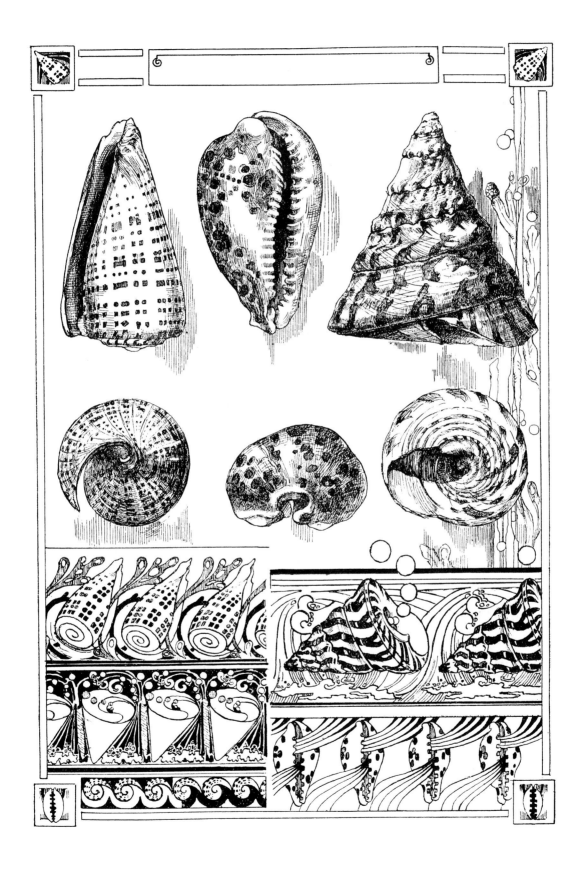

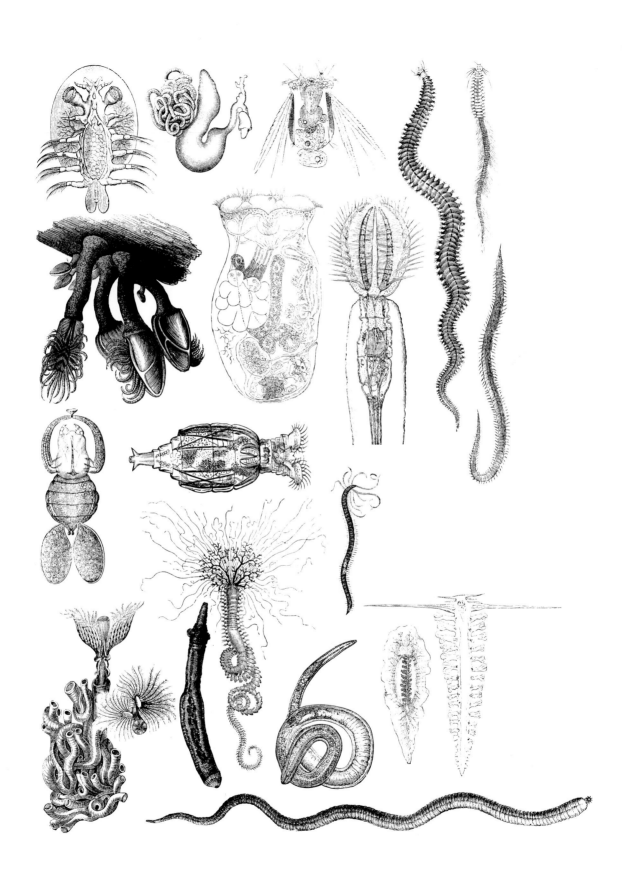

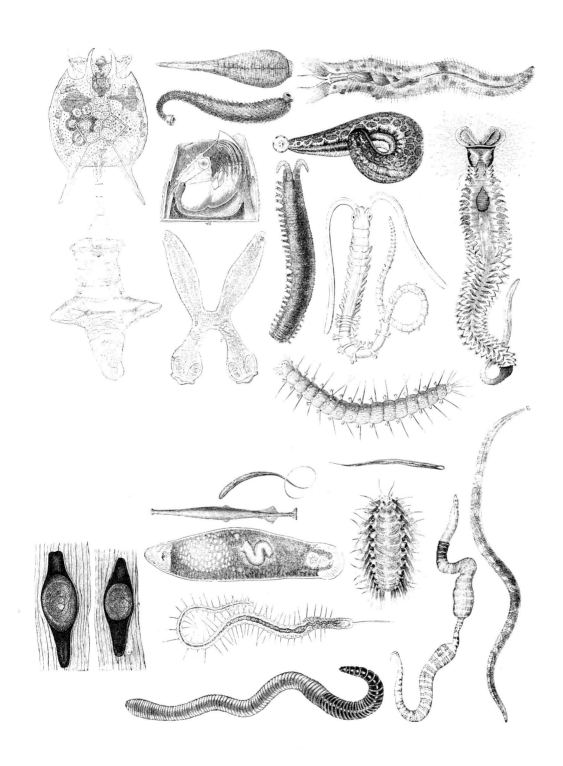

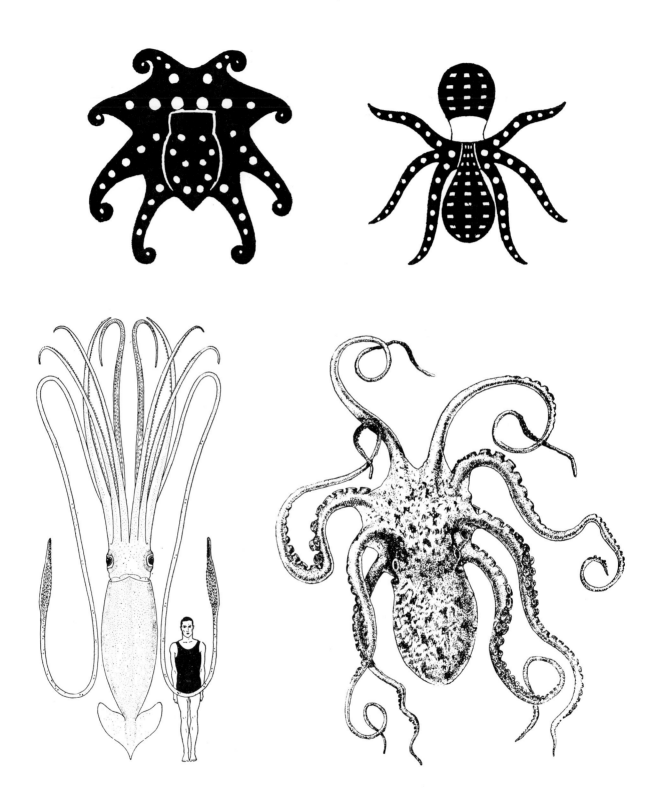

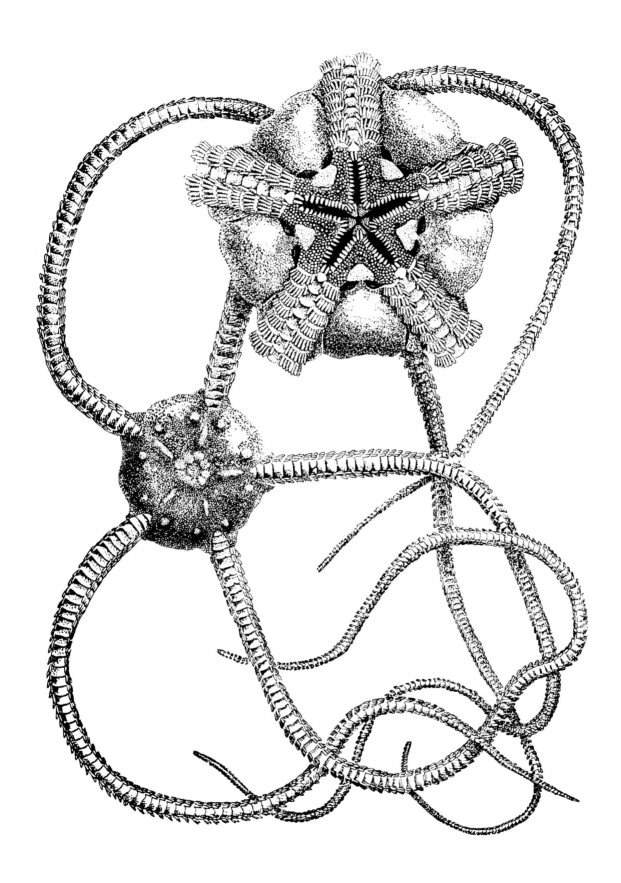

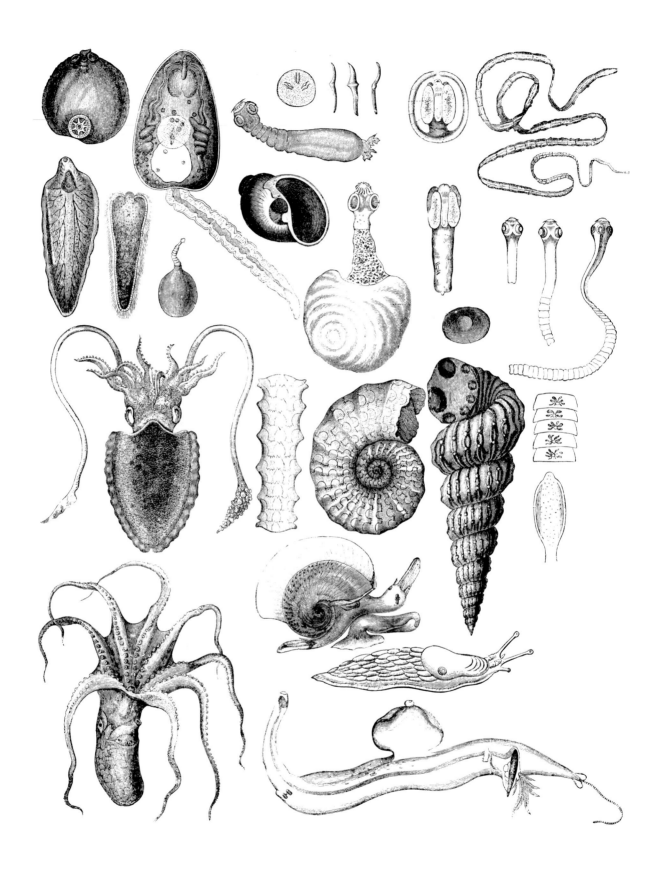

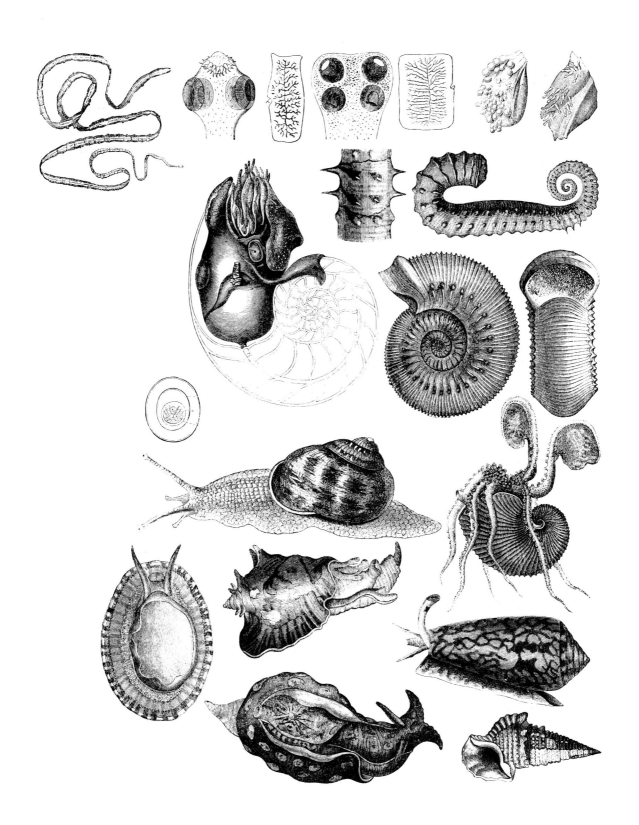

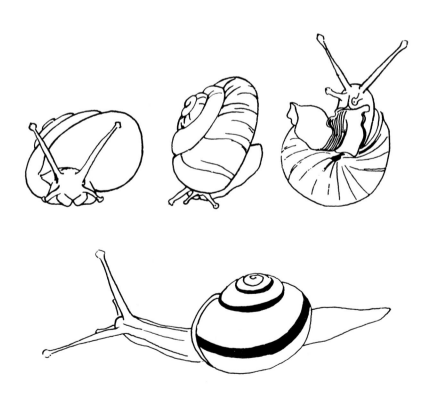

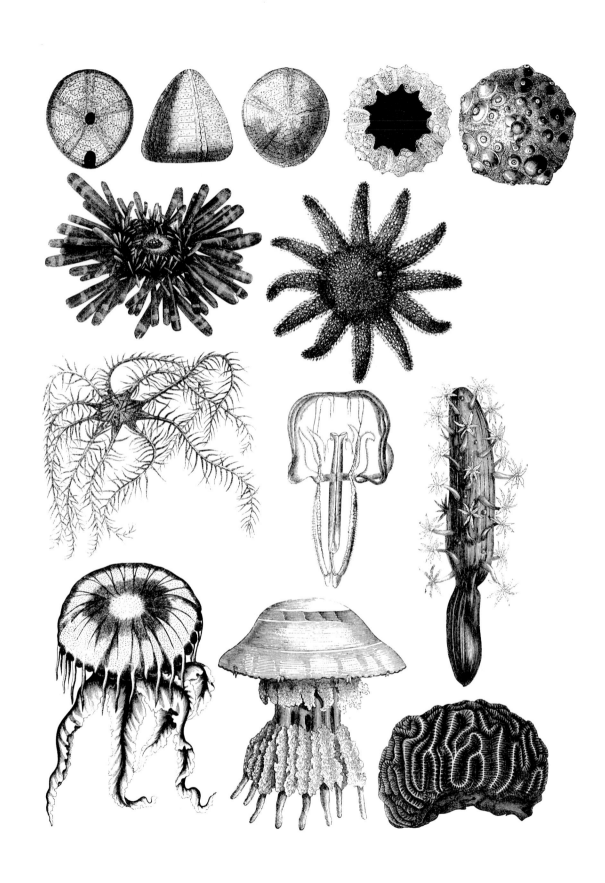

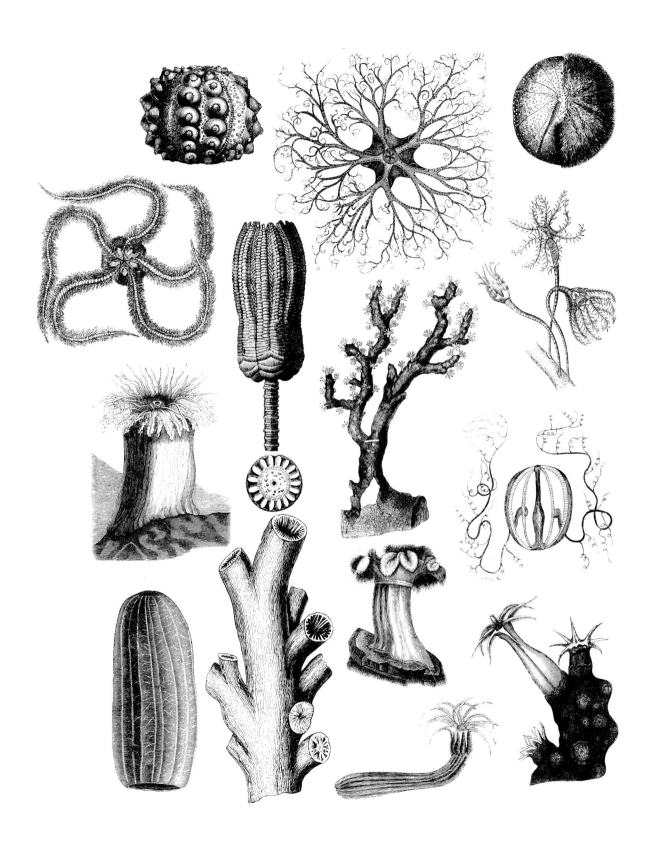

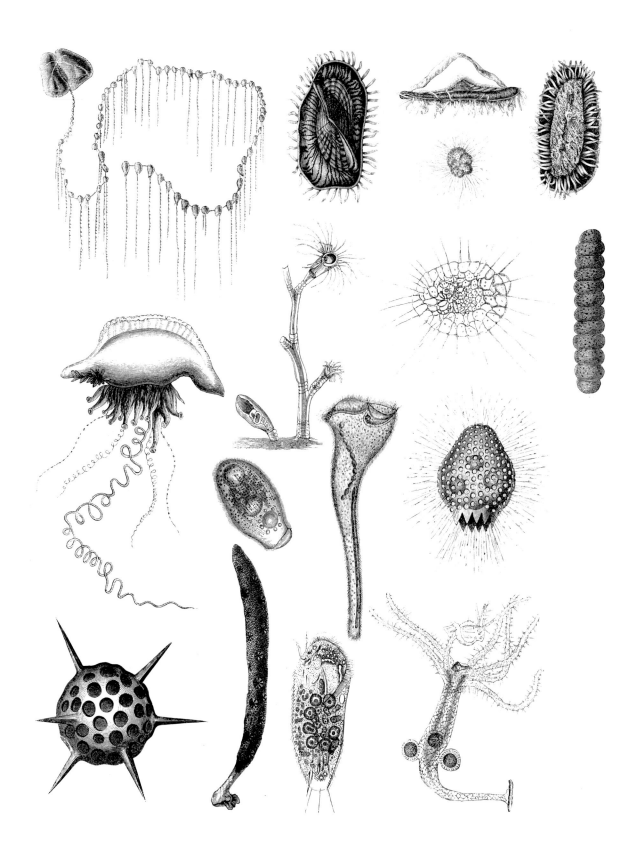

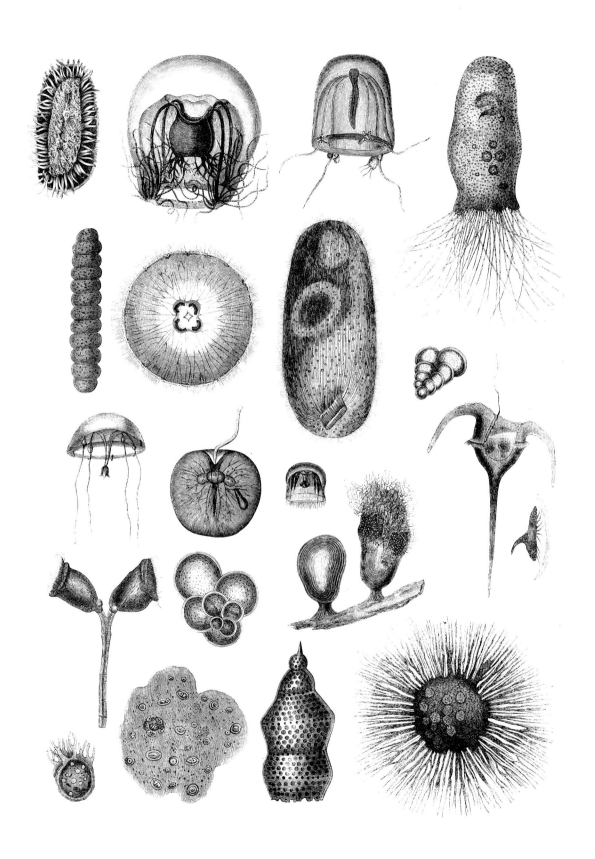